# LOVE IS ALL THERE IS

**THE REST WE MADE UP**

Rev. Dr. George Harris

Love Is All There Is

Copyright © 2023 by Wise Woman Press

All rights reserved. No part of this book may be used or reproduced in any form whatsoever without written permission except in the case of brief quotations in critical articles or reviews.

Printed in the United States of America.

For more information, or to book an event, contact :
(George Harris )  famlivsys@spinn.net

ISBN 978-0-945385-91-2

First Edition March 2023

# Dedications

This book is dedicated to a wonderful couple Gordon and Maureen Dudley, who joined me in creating a "Purple" building that we were in as neighbors.

Purple is a political term meaning Blue and Red mixed together. When they moved in, we made a great connection, and then I found out they were strong gun-toting, Trump backers, Republican Conservatives.

And of course, I am a Liberal Democrat, hate guns, and am not a fan of Trump. So, one day I talked to them saying that we would see each other constantly since we lived next door and I didn't want anything to get in the way, I told them I was a Minister of Peace and I just wanted love between us, and they agreed. And from there on, we just expressed love for each other and didn't let our individual beliefs get in the way by discussing them.

They have since moved about 1 hour away and we are still friends, get together for lunch and still express love to each other when we get together. We created what this book is about. Thank you, Gordon and Maureen.

My second dedication is to Ginny Andrews who is a real close friend and was with me when I started this book and supported me in its' completion. She also helped with editing when I was finished. Without her help and support, this book would never have been finished. Deep thanks to you Ginny for your love and insights.

# Table of Contents

Forward .......................................................................................................... 1

Lesson 1  The Man Who Did Not Believe In God!!!!! (Anonymous) ..................... 5

Lesson 2  Laborless Love ................................................................................ 13

Lesson 3  What Is Love? ................................................................................ 17

Lesson 4  What Is Love? (Part II) ................................................................... 20

Lesson 5  Is God Enough? .............................................................................. 25

Lesson 6  You Are Love ................................................................................. 33

Lesson 7  4 Bodies Of God ............................................................................. 39

Lesson 8  Being The Solution ......................................................................... 48

Lesson 9  Being Alone With The Beloved ........................................................ 58

Lesson 10  The Power Of Commitment To God ............................................... 62

Lesson 11  What Does God See? .................................................................... 66

Lesson-12  Raising Your Vibrational Rate ....................................................... 72

Lesson 13  Practicing The Presence ................................................................ 76

Lesson 14  Everything Is Energy .................................................................... 78

Lesson 15  Awakened Heart ........................................................................... 81

Lesson 16  Identifying Grace As It Flows Thru Us ........................................... 86

Lesson 17  Love Makes The World Go Round ................................................. 93

Lesson 18  Channeling God ............................................................................ 97

Lesson 19  "Our Journey Of Freedom To Love" ............................................. 101

Lesson 20  Our Journey Of Love .................................................................. 105

Lesson 21  Is It Love Or Fantasy? ................................................................ 112

Lesson 22  I Am Here For You!! ................................................................... 120

Lesson 23  "Seeing Thru The Eyes Of God .................................................... 129

Lesson 24  New Year Thoughts .................................................................... 138

Lesson 25  A Moment Of Christhood ................................................................. 141

Lesson 26  Battle Of The Wills .......................................................................... 147

Lesson 27  I Am A Magnificent, Unique And Radiantaspect Of The Divine .... 154

Lesson 28  Miscellaneous *I Walk With God In Perfect Holiness* .......................... 162

Prayer Treatments ............................................................................................ 164

Love (Emmet Fox) ............................................................................................. 164

New "Our Father" ............................................................................................ 165

Defining Love (Christina Tilla) ......................................................................... 166

The Rhythm Of God Daily Meditation ............................................................. 167

Practicing The Presence (Joel Goldsmith) ....................................................... 169

Contract ............................................................................................................ 170

# LOVE IS ALL THERE IS, THE REST WE MADE UP
## Forward

The most talked about, debated, misunderstood topic in our society is GOD. So many descriptions and judgments of God have been portrayed and written about over the years, including the infamous statement "God is Dead" by the Beatles. And since God is Love, in my belief, we have numerous mistaken ideas of what Love is as well.

You are killing more of each other every day over your quarrels about religion than all other things put together because you cannot even come to an agreement about what you think God says or wants for you. On one side of the world, God wants something different than the other.

On one side of the room, in one side of your mind, God wants something different than on the other. The truth is that you are extensions of this powerful source energy that I call the love and loveliness of God. This means that you are literally God expressing in this physical body.

And so, as you are standing in a thought, a word, or an action that feels good to you, then you are fully open and allowing all that Divine Energy to flow through you. And in that moment, you are all that you said you would be when you decided to come forth into this body.

"You are the extension of pure positive energy. You are in your full creative power. You are thriving. You are clear-minded. You are joyful. You are filled with love. You are who you are, you are allowing that which you really are. And you are seeing more of what life is." –Abraham

That is what this book is about, and I know that you will receive benefit from it to help you realize and live all that was written in that above statement by Abraham. I have an asterisk at the end of the title on the front of the book. The reason for that is I need to give credit to Rev Patrick Pollard.

He was Minister of the "Albuquerque Center of Spiritual Living" which I attended, for 10 or so years and Rev. Patrick used that statement a lot and I love the truth of it. The idea of God has evolved over the ages, but there are still people who hold onto old ancient ideas of God. Mainly around God being a judgmental, vindictive, fearful, father figure that sits on a throne and passes judgment over all souls. And we are told we are sinners. No wonder we have such problems and issues with earthly fathers.

Because of humans' different versions of God, Deepak Chopra wrote a book titled "How to Know God- The Soul's Journey into the Mystery of Mysteries." In it, he describes The Stages of God, as man has seen over time. They are God the Protector, God the Almighty, God of Peace, God the Redeemer, God the Creator, God of Miracles, and lastly the God of Pure Being- "I AM." That God is the one I will write about in this book. And you will notice that throughout the book I have put the words I AM in caps for that reason. I highly recommend his book for some understanding of God over the centuries.

There are a few reasons why I AM writing this book. First, back in 2010 I entered a contest titled" The Next Great Visionary Author," which was created by a teacher/friend of mine, and author of many books, James Twyman. I didn't get far in the competition. It wasn't because of the topic but because of the steps involved that I couldn't get together in time. It was the beginning of this book you are now reading. The purpose of this book was to include some of the talks I have given at my two churches over the years about God and Love.

You'll notice it has been 11 years since I got back to it. Sometimes things take a while to percolate and grow before actual manifestation according to the Universal Law of Divine Timing. Second, this book is written from a spiritual aspect of who I AM—a Minister of Metaphysics, New Thought, and Spiritual Peacemaking.

Also, because right now to me, that seems to be the highest understanding of who and what God is and especially how God loves you. Since I became a pulpit minister, on the guidance of God, I have talked about that topic so much in my church that it helped the subject grow within me with deeper understanding.

As it has grown deeper in me, I have realized how all of us have or are currently suffering from some level of lack of self-love, as God loves us. And when I felt it, I comprehended why we have so many problems in this world and why we need to get back to deep love of self.

That will come from God within us and our connection to the Christ Consciousness. Third, some time ago in meditation I was given these two statements: 1) I'm fully engaged as a Spiritual Being and now serve mankind as an example. 2) My mission, therefore, is to wake up as many people as possible to the power of Love.

That has been the guiding force in my service work to the world. I have experienced both sides, strong lack of self-love from an abusive childhood and a deep level of Self-Love in connection to Source/God/Spirit. And so now I choose Self-Love. That one always has felt better to me and as a result I AM aware of when others are in lack of self-love. And I hold the place of Love to help them get there themselves. My hope is that this book will help you connect to your deeper understanding and the experience of self-love. How sweet it is.

Since I have had visions about success of this book and even other books that I will complete at some future date, I feel totally blessed by it. Affirmation: *I state now that this book will be a best seller, bringing me financial prosperity.*

I will facilitate workshops as well as hold private sessions with people on this subject. Along with that I will BE a speaker on tour about this important subject; and teach a course in college and high school on what LOVE is. I will use information from Source and experience the highest level of God's love in myself. I will connect to, live, and express my mission on a deep level and the past of lack/separation is gone from me. Therefore, my Oneness with God is now alive. Anything is possible in our lives by loving ourselves. And, to you as the reader, you may want to write out a goal for you to attract to you through your deeper love. And of course, in this book, Love and God are interchangeable. Come join me in a deepening journey of self-love, to SEE How God LOVES.

That is the focus, and we'll start with a story about fear of Love, and then go through many steps as lessons to reach the final lesson which is about how MAgnificent You are.

NAMASTE, I Love You and You are Loved

# Lesson 1
# THE MAN WHO DID NOT BELIEVE IN GOD!!!!!
## (Anonymous)

This was an ordinary man, just like you and me, but what made this man different was his way of thinking. He thought that love didn't exist. Of course, he had a lot of experience trying to find love, and he had observed the people around him. Much of his life had been spent searching for love, only to find that love didn't exist.

Wherever this man went, he used to tell people that love is nothing, but an invention of the poets, an invention of religions just to manipulate the weak minds of humans, to have control over humans, to make them believe. He said love is not real, and that's why no human could ever find love, even though he might look for it.

This man was highly intelligent, and he was very convincing. He read a lot of books and went to the best universities, and he became a respected scholar. Of course, he was living in his mind totally ignoring the heart. He could stand in any public place, in front of any kind of people, and his logic was strong. What he said was that love is just like a drug; it makes you very high, but it creates a strong need. You can become highly addicted to love, but what happens when you don't receive your daily doses of love? Just like a drug, you need your everyday doses.

He used to say that most relationships between lovers are like a relationship between a drug addict and the one who provides the drugs. The one who has the biggest need is like the drug addict; the one who has a little need is like the provider. The one who has the little need is the one who controls the whole relationship. You can see this dynamic so clearly.

This is because, usually in every relationship, there is one who loves the most, and the other who doesn't love, who only takes advantage of the one who gives his or her heart. You can see the way they manipulate each other, their actions, and reactions, and they are just like the provider and the addict.

The drug addict, the one who has the biggest need, lives in constant fear that perhaps he will not be able to get the next dosage of love or the drug. The drug addict thinks, "What am I going to do if he/she leaves me?" That fear makes the drug addict very possessive.

"That's mine!" The addict becomes jealous and demanding because of the fear of not having the next dosage. The provider can control and manipulate the one who needs the drug by giving more doses, fewer doses, or no doses at all. The one, who has the biggest need, completely surrenders, and will do whatever he can to avoid being abandoned.

The man went on explaining to everyone why love doesn't exist. "What humans call "love" is nothing, but a fear relationship based on control. Where is the respect? Where is the love they claim to have? There is no love.

Young couples, in front of the representation of God, in front of their family and friends, make a lot of promises to each other: to live together forever, to love and respect each other, to be there for each other, through the good times and the bad times.

They promise to love and honor each other and make promises and more promises. What is amazing is that they really believe these promises. But after the marriage—one week later, a month later, a few months later—you can see that none of these promises are kept.

What you find is a war of control to see who will manipulate whom. Who will be the provider, and who will have the addiction? You will find that a few months later, the respect they swear to have for each other is gone.

You can see the resentment, the emotional poison, how they hurt each other, little by little, and it grows and grows, until they don't know when the love stops. They stay together because they are afraid to be alone, afraid of the opinions and judgments of others, and afraid of their own judgments and opinions. But where is the love?"

He used to claim that he saw many old couples that had lived together thirty, forty, fifty years, and they were so proud to have lived together all those years. But when they talked about their relationship, what they said was, "We survived the matrimony."

That means one of them surrendered to the other; at a certain time, he/she gave up and decided to endure the suffering. The one with the strongest will and less need won the war, but where is the flame they call love? They treat each other like a possession: "She is mine." "He is mine."

The man went on and on about all the reasons why he believed love doesn't exist, and he told others, "I have done all of that already. I will no longer allow anyone to manipulate my mind and control my life in the name of love." His arguments were quite logical, and he convinced many people by all his words, love doesn't exist.

Then one day, this man was walking in a park, and there on a bench was a beautiful lady who was crying. When he saw her crying, he felt curiosity. Sitting beside her, he asked if he could help her. He asked why she was crying. You can imagine his surprise when she told him, she was crying because love doesn't exist.

He said, "This is amazing—a woman who believes that love doesn't exist!" Of course, he wanted to know more about her. "Why do you say that love doesn't exist?" He asked. "Well, it's a long story," she replied. "I married when I was very young, with all of the love, all these illusions, full of hope that I would share my life with this man.

We swore to each other our loyalty, respect, and honor, and we created a family. But soon everything changed. I was the devoted wife who took care of the children, and the home. My husband continued to develop his career and his success and image outside of home was more important to him than our family.

He lost respect for me, and I lost respect for him. We hurt each other, and at a certain point I discovered that I didn't love him, and he didn't love me either. But the children needed a father, and that was my excuse to stay and do whatever I could to support him.

Now the children are grown, and they have left. I no longer have any excuse to stay with him. There is no respect; there's no kindness. I know that even if I find someone else, it's going to be the same, because love doesn't exist. There is no sense to look around for something that doesn't exist.

That is why I am crying. "Understanding her very well, he embraced her and said, "You are right; love doesn't exist. We look for love, we open our heart and we become vulnerable, just to find selfishness that hurts us even if we don't think we will be hurt.

It doesn't matter how many relationships we have, the same thing happens again and again. Why even search for love any longer?" They were so much alike, and they became the best friends ever. It was a wonderful relationship. They respected each other, and they never put each other down.

With each step they took together, they were happy. There was no envy or jealousy, there was no control, and there was no possessiveness. They were living in the heart. The relationship kept growing and growing. They loved to be together, because when they were together, they had a lot of fun.

When they were not together, they missed each other. One day when the man was out of town, he had the weirdest idea. He was thinking, "HMMM, maybe what I feel for her is love. But this is so different from what I have ever felt before. It's not what the poets say it is, it's not what the religions say it is.

That is because I am not responsible for her. I don't take anything from her. I don't have the need for her to take care of me. I don't need to blame her for my difficulties or to take my dramas to her. We have the best time together; we enjoy each other. I respect the way she thinks, the way she feels.

She doesn't embarrass me; she doesn't bother me at all. I don't feel jealous when she is with other people. I don't feel any envy when she is successful. Perhaps love does exist, but it's not what everyone thinks love is. He could hardly wait to go back home and talk to her, to let her know about his weird idea.

As soon as he started talking, she said, "I know exactly what you are talking about. I had the same idea long ago, but I didn't want to share it with you because I know you don't believe in love. Perhaps love does exist, but it isn't what we thought it was." They decided to become lovers and to live together, and it was amazing that things didn't change. They still respected each other; they were still supportive of each other, and the love grew more and more. Even the simplest things made their hearts sing with love because they were so happy.

The man's heart was so full of all of the love he felt that one night a great miracle happened. He was looking at the stars and he found the most beautiful one, and his love was so big that the star started coming down from the sky and soon the star was in his hands.

Then a second miracle happened, and his soul merged with that star. He was intensely happy, and he could hardly wait to go to the woman and put the star in her hands to prove his love to her. As soon as he put the star in her hands, she felt a moment of doubt.

This love was overwhelming, she wasn't sure she was worthy of it, and in that moment, the star fell from her hands and broke into a million pieces. Now there is an old man walking around the world swearing that love doesn't exist.

And there is a beautiful old woman at home waiting for a man, shedding a tear for a paradise that once she had in her hands, but for a moment of doubt, she let it go. This is the story of the man who didn't believe in love. That probably sounds somewhat depressing.

Yet there is lots of truth in that story and there are a few questions to be asked. In the beginning, when the old man told his reason for why Love doesn't exist, how many of you have had similar thoughts going on, or remembered that in the past you believed those thoughts?

How many of you have experienced that form of control around love, or have experienced someone who has? If our thoughts create our reality around us, what thoughts of his attracted that situation to him?

Even though it sounds depressing, it's quite familiar of how some of us as humans experience love. And then towards the end, why do you think that it happened the way it did? Especially after the joy and love they seemed to have experienced?

Most likely because of how long and how strong had they carried thoughts that LOVE didn't exist? And even though if felt different, it is not easy to rid oneself of those negative thoughts, especially when you project them on someone else.

That is the problem, looking for someone outside of yourself, to receive love from. Because she was still connected to her human part, she felt unworthy. And because both were connected to their ego, they didn't believe in love. Being unworthy is a strong thought and emotion that most of us still carry around.

"We haven't yet experienced the truth about worthiness, which contrary to popular thinking; isn't something you earn, it's something you recognize, in you. And once you do, you won't be able to think, speak, or behave in any other way than as if what you most wanted was meant to be. You were born worthy, The Universe. "(Give thanks to TUT- The Universe Talks- Mike Dooley)

The Truth is LOVE is grand, it is magnificent; it is like ONE. I just wrote, it's the size of this room, even bigger. The whole universe holds this Love for us. LOVE helps empower people; it feeds one if they can take it inside for themselves, to experience GOD within themselves because GOD is LOVE.

And as I said in the title, and again, all there is, is Love, the rest we made up; therefore, the rest is just an illusion. There is no Love but God's Love.

NAMASTE, I Love You and You are Loved

# Fellowship of Spirit Talk
# 3/15/14)
# Lesson 2
# LABORLESS LOVE

*"There is a Light in you which cannot die."*

In this moment, I Give All Glory to God. Here is another story about LOVE, more positive: The story goes that some time ago, a man punished his 5-year-old daughter for wasting a roll of expensive gold wrapping paper. Money was tight and he became even more upset when the child pasted the gold paper to decorate a box to put under the Christmas tree.

Nevertheless, the little girl brought the gift box to her father the next morning and said, "This is for you, Daddy." The father was embarrassed by his earlier overreaction, but his anger flared again when he found the box was empty. He spoke to her in a harsh manner.

"Don't you know, young lady, when you give someone a present, there's supposed to be something inside the package? The little girl looked up at him with tears in her eyes and said: "Daddy, it's not empty. I blew kisses into it until it was full." The father was crushed. He fell on his knees and put his arms around his little girl, and he begged her to forgive him for his unnecessary anger.

An accident took the life of the child only a short time later and it is told that the father kept that gold box by his bed for all the years of his life. And whenever he was discouraged or faced difficult problems, he would open the box and take out an imaginary kiss and remember the love of the child who had put it there. (Anonymous)

In a very real sense, each of us as human beings have been given a golden box filled with unconditional love and kisses from our mothers, family, friends, and God. There is no more precious possession anyone could hold. So, what was the difference between those two stories?

How did LOVE manifest itself, more so in the 2nd story? Each of you has your answers that work for you. And I would say it manifested because it came from the child's heart. unconditionally, without expectation, or fear. It seems as if there are two kinds of love.

When we are trying to manipulate circumstances, ourselves, or each other, there is the kind of love that seems like hard work, filled with strain and struggle. When we try to make people do what we want out of our "love" for them, it's always with a great effort. We feel tired of trying so hard to get them to understand us or to change their ways toward us. Because we want them to grow, we become anxious for results—we want to see that they are really getting somewhere—at least from our point of view.

Nothing is so impatient as watching our loved one's lack of progress on the spiritual path. That's one kind of love: love with effort. The other kind of love is to love those releases and let go. This is a freeing kind of love—effortless, laborless love. The kind of love the little girl in the story lived.

As we come to love the people and situations in our life from a perspective of setting everyone free, then love ceases to be a struggle. There are no conditions for our love of God, ourselves, another person, or life itself. We simply love. This love imposes no demands, restrictions, or requirements.

This love is based on our recognition of the oneness's of all life; we all breathe the same air; we all share the same time and space; we all inhabit this gentle earth together. No need to struggle to get them to see that our way is best for them. We let go in trust that God in them is as wise as God within all of us.

And we also learn to trust ourselves more and more as we let go to effortless love. There is no more of God in the most enlightened person on the planet than there is in us. We belong to the inextricable web of love that connects all life everywhere. We're at home in God in love—so we can relax.

The way of the heart is the way of love. Love brings us by a way we know not to where we need to be in this life. Love guides our feet to find our path of bliss. Love guides our minds to illumination and our souls to God. Who do we love in this life? There, we find God's Presence, God's Goodness and God's Grace.

A woman once came to the great Indian yogi, Ramakrishna, and said, "I cannot love God." The yogi remained silent for a moment. Then he asked, 'Is there anyone in this life you do love?" I love my little son, the woman replied. There," he said. "There is God." Love lights our way through this life.

Love releases us from the path of our longing. As we open our hearts to Love, the Universe suddenly fills us with a joy that we never felt before, and we see a beauty that we never saw before. Everyone and everything take on a new radiance as we see them through the eyes of love.

And as we listen with Love's ears, we hear the music of stars. Love transforms our earth into wonder. Love heals our past and brings joy to our future. There is no path to Love! Love Itself is the path. Let's let this be the place and the season of love. (Rev Larry Morris)

### RISE TO ADORE THE MYSTERY OF LOVE

Love's Light shines thru you

Love's smile brightens you

Love's breath livens you

Love's Life lives you and you,

You are that Love

Love's pulse pounds in your heart

Love's grace surrounds you

Love's pace astounds you

Love's Life gives you

For Love's Life lives you

NAMASTE, I Love You and You are Loved

# Fellowship of Spirit Talk
## 2/14/16
## Lesson 3
### WHAT IS LOVE?

The Light in you is what the Universe longs to behold.

In this moment, I Give all Glory to God. I know that everyone has different ideas of what Love is, as well as different interpretations of practically every word in the dictionary. If we are going to understand how God loves us and allow that love into us, we need to understand the varied topics of Love on a higher plane or level.

Let's start with the normal human understanding of Love. As humans, we set aside one day we to acknowledge Love, and that is Valentine's Day. And we have some people that really get into it and others that believe it is just a marketing scam to sell things and ask why we don't have it all year long.

Well, we do as a continuing possibility since we are all BEINGS of Love. It is always a choice to acknowledge the love of your partner, love of yourself and especially and most importantly your love of God. And if we chose, we could celebrate that way every day.

Just because we don't and just have that one day to celebrate doesn't mean that it is not real. And of course, we do have other people, who are single and who do not have a partner to share that day with. But again, that is not a reason to not have a day of celebration, a day of personal spiritual love.

I would state here that the deeper truth is, whether you have a partner with you or not, you can still celebrate that day as a day of self-love. That is because your partner is always you and GOD in

Oneness of God's LOVE, Unconditional Love, the ultimate truth of who we all are.

It is an opportunity to Love yourself as deeply as you can. The issue though is that we all suffer from some sort of lack of self-love, which is why this book was written. As an idea to include everyone, we ought to celebrate like we did when we were children.

That is to give valentines to ALL the kids in the room, all of those in our lives and receive back a valentine from everyone. By doing that we would be acknowledging Love and each other more. But then again, people would find something to complain about such as the cost of valentines or flowers or whatever you might buy. So be it.

Of course, on a spiritual level, we understand complaining to be FEAR. And we want to talk about the opposite, which is LOVE. So, what is love? We say things like, I love chocolate, I love sunsets, I love Italian food, and so many other things. We say to our parents, our children, our friends, I LOVE YOU.

And then we say to our partners, spouses, lovers, I LOVE YOU. We may say those words differently, depending on whom they are spoken to. Then of course, how often is it that later down the road, we say the opposite, I don't love you anymore or I hate you.

How easy those words and emotions can change. And that is because it is human love, not God's Divine Love. For some of us the question remains, Is it the same love or a different one? I believe it is the same, since there is only one Love, God's. The difference is whether we are talking from our heart or our ego mind.

As a practice, what if you looked around the room you are in right now and you looked at it as nothing but Love. How much would you feel of it? And what would it feel like to you? Another practice relating to self-love, on a scale of 0-10, where would you place yourself regarding all these aspects of your life?

Prosperity or Financial Independence, Health, Self-Esteem, Self-Worth, Self-Love, Self-Confidence, Loving Relationships, Career or Good Paying Job, Liking What You're Doing, Time to Enjoy Life, and finally Spiritually Nurtured—I bet you never looked at these categories relating to Love.

But they are important as they all influence us. And if you do not have a high level (10) of love for self in each category, I would state that you are lacking in SELF-LOVE. I created and taught a class titled "Practicing the Presence" about these qualities. We need to practice continually.

That means that we don't have it totally handled, we are still practicing the presence of God within. And the 10 aspects named above are part of the whole of life that needs to BE loved. When we look at love, it should start with ourselves, then God and then others. If we are lacking in our own self-love, then we do not have enough in the next 2 categories: God, and others.

NAMASTE, I Love You and You are Loved

# Fellowship of Spirit Talk
# 2/21/16
# Lesson 4
# WHAT IS LOVE? (Part II)

*All things that live bring gifts to you in gratitude.*

In this moment I Give All Glory to God. So, what is Love? WE explored that question in the last lesson. Let's go deeper by sharing 6 statements with you and see how they fit.

Taking the letters: L O V E

L = listen to what is being said.
O = observe the other person and their feelings.
V = voice your acknowledgment that you're actively listening.
E = express yourself in a meaningful way.
LOVE could also mean: "Living on Vibrational Energy"

We need oxygen, food, and water to live. What if we were co-creating with God as he has asked, and just lived on the high vibrational energy of God's Love, knowing that we were being taken care of? I can just imagine most people reacting to that statement out of fear.

I certainly did before I understood the truth. Let's look over each one for further explanation.

L = Listen to what is being said. That is a difficult step to take in relationships, as we tend to keep thinking in our mind how we want to reply to the other. If the Christ lives in each other, listening is an important truth to live by. When listening we might be surprised by what the other says.

O = Observe the other person and their feelings/emotions. In my work our thoughts, words and actions come under Love (feelings) or Fear (emotions). To treat ourselves and each other with love means we need to connect to the other and be aware of their emotions/feelings as well as our own.

V = Voice your acknowledgment that you're actively listening. Everyone wants to be heard and it is important. Communication is one of two top aspects of life, the other being relationship. As spiritual beings we need to improve ourselves in those two categories to create our life with God.

E = Express yourself in a meaningful way. Again, looking at the aspect of communication we need to stop blame and attack which are the two worst blocks to positive communication. To accomplish that we need to watch the language we use and the words we express that are not of Love and God.

LOVE could also mean: "Living on Vibrational Energy." If we practice just those tools, although I have many more to use, we create the space in our relationships to live in a higher level of vibration called LOVE and ONENESS, treating ourselves and others as the Christ that we are. To continue:

2) "LOVE is the place you are coming from, your ground of BEING, you are Love." How powerful to know that truth and live it.

3) "LOVE is the Divine force everywhere, the Universal energy moving power of Love that flows in your own heart." Just imagine how your life would be living this truth.

4) "LOVE is accepting yourself first and then someone else as he or she is." And as he or she is not. How easy is that? If it were, life would be a lot more fulfilling. But remember, we all are the Christ.

5) "LOVE is the acknowledgment of a union that already exists." All right, Love is not something we need to work for, it is already in us as who we are.

6) LOVE is the space we give to each other, to BE who we are. There you go, we need to just BE the truth of who we are in every situation of our lives and let GOD take care of the DOING. More points to consider about Self-Love—living your life as GOD!

Acknowledging and praising yourself verbally to yourself

Approving of all your actions

Having confidence in your ability

Loving your body and admiring your beauty

Giving yourself pleasure without guilt

Giving yourself what you want and feeling you deserve it

Letting yourself win

Letting others in instead of submitting to loneliness

Following your own intuition

Making your own rules responsibly

Seeking your own perfection

Taking credit for what you did

Surrounding yourself with beauty

Letting yourself be rich and not staying in poverty

Creating an abundance of friends

Rewarding yourself, never punishing yourself

Trusting yourself

Nourishing yourself with good food and ideas

Surrounding yourself with people who nourish you

Enjoying sex

Getting a massage frequently

Seeing yourself as equal to others

Forgiving yourself

Letting in affection

Authority over yourself, not giving it away to others

Developing your creative abilities

Having fun all the time

Really talking to yourself gently and lovingly

Becoming your own approving inner parent

Turning all your negative thoughts into affirmations.

These all by themselves could be in a book by itself. They came from Sondra Ray, breath worker and author. Take some time to look them over and write down the ones you don't have and would like to, especially the ones you felt a reaction in your body around.

Do meditation on connecting the energy of each one of these. Notice how you feel and where in your body to feel the reaction. We talk about unconditional Love, maybe not understanding what it means. So here are some steps to take on how to Love yourself unconditionally as God loves you:

Stop all criticism: It never changes a thing. Refuse to criticize yourself. Accept yourself exactly as you are. When you approve of yourself, change is positive.

Don't scare yourself: Stop terrorizing yourself with your thoughts. It's a dreadful way to live. Find a mental image that gives you pleasure.

BE Gentle, Kind, Patient: Do that for yourself. Learn new ways of thinking. Trust yourself as you would someone you really loved.

Be kind to your mind. Self-hatred is only hating your own thoughts which are the ego's thoughts. Just change the thoughts.

Praise Yourself: Criticism breaks down the spirit. Praise builds it up. Praise yourself as much as you can.

Support yourself: Find ways to support yourself Reach out to friends and allow them to help you.

BE loving to Your Negatives: Acknowledge that you created them to fulfill a need. Now, you are finding positive ways to fulfill those needs.

Take care of your body: Learn about nutrition. Learn about exercise. Cherish the temple you live in.

Mirror work: Look into your eyes often. Express the growing sense of love you have for yourself. At least once a day say "I LOVE YOU."

DO IT NOW: Begin now. DO YOUR BEST. We are divine beings, and we are also human. As such we have a lot of human traits to become aware of and change so that we live our lives on earth as the true BEINGS that we are. This lesson of tools should go a long way to help you all BEcome your highest truth.

NAMASTE, I Love You and You are Loved

# Fellowship of Spirit Talk
# 6/29/14
# Lesson 5
# IS GOD ENOUGH?

*The scent of flowers is their gift to you.*

In this moment, I Give all Glory to God! Beloved's, as I have said before, LOVE is All there is, the rest we made up. That statement says it all, doesn't it? Okay, here are a few jokes about children asking God questions:

Dear God: Instead of letting people die, and having to make new ones, why don't you just keep the ones you have now? (Jane)

Dear God: Thank you for my baby brother, but what I prayed for was a puppy. (Joyce)

Dear God: I bet it is very hard for you to love everybody in the whole world. There are only 4 people in our family, and I can never do it. (Nan)

First, the title of this lesson sounds as if we ought to explore the question: Is there only God? Or are there other things that might be more enough than God. A statue, lots of money, power, etc. We'll explore that in this lesson.

If we want to claim that Love is all there is and God is Love, so God is all there is. God is also our Good, so Good is all there is.

As a friend of mine says when asked if he believes in a God." No, I believe only in God." Of course, there would be those who would say: "I haven't received my good yet or I have had nothing but bad things happen to me. So, how could Good be all there is?"

We also say that God is in everything, you, me, everything in the world, as everything comes from God. And if that is true, then all there is, is God. Think about that, in all the Universe, GOD is all there is. Of course, people ask other questions: "If there is nothing but God, then why is there such pain and suffering in the world?"

Why is there lack, war, abuse, anger, hatred? If God is everything, is that enough? In the past, lots of civilizations created false Gods, believing that there had to be more than this so-called God that wasn't even seen, just talked about.

I guess the thought was, wouldn't it be better if there was a God we could see, touch, talk to, something that looked more real. SO, we started giving ourselves our power to something out there, believing that it would be enough for us. And ever since then we have continued giving our power to something "Out there" outside of ourselves.

And that is because we are looking for something to fill that empty space, we feel inside of ourselves. The space right here in our heart. Let's explore some of those other things we give our power to, i.e. money and make it "Bad" or "Good." And so, I ask the question, "Is money enough?"

Does having money give us all the happiness, and joy we desire? NO! We have all been ruled by money or I should say by our thoughts about money. Either we have enough, or we don't have enough. And then we either feel enough or not enough based on money.

I remember a friend who got paid once a month at end of the month. In the beginning of the month when she had money, she was o.k., but the last week or so before receiving her pay she was in a negative mood of fear, and when she then received her check, everything was o.k.

Does money give us all the Love, Peace and Joy that we desire inside? NO! So, apparently, Money is not enough, in and of itself. What about relationships? We give ourselves to the false God of relationship, believing that someone else, a partner, will give us what we desire.

Has relationship been enough? NO, not always, especially when the divorce rate is above 50% for 1st marriages and climbing higher for 2nd marriages. We get into a relationship believing that this someone else will make us feel loved, special, all those feelings that we have all been wanting to experience.

But we look outside to bring it to us. And then somewhere down the road we find out we are still unhappy, but we blame the other person for it and try to find someone else to give us what we are looking for. So apparently relationship is not enough in and of itself.

Especially since we have disconnected from our relationship to God. What about our jobs? We take on jobs or careers, believing that somehow, we will be happy, well paid, acknowledged for the wonderful employee we are and the great work we do.

And we give our power away to this job or the boss, believing that they have more power than we do. Then we end up spending 8 hrs. a day or more doing something that really doesn't satisfy us the way we want. Either we stay there for the security or again we go looking for another one that will help us feel good, give us what we want.

But usually at the end of the day we are tired, stressed and maybe barely have time to spend with our mate, whom we said were the ones that would give us the joy we wanted, in the first place. I do mediation for child custody cases, so when couples separate or divorce, they must mediate and create a parenting plan.

One couple I remember came to me to create a plan. They had a son about 4 or 5, and the father worked in the oil field which took him away a whole lot. Now they are divorcing, and he was rarely home before and now he had to figure out the times to have his son by himself.

During the meeting he got angry and said "I did everything for you I was supposed to. I bought you a house and a car." And she said, "Yes, but I felt like I was in the 50's, you were rarely home." Both parties had different views of relationship and never talked about them.

So apparently, jobs are not enough, in and of themselves. What about children? Lots of women and men have children because they want to be loved or have something to give their love to. Not knowing that it should be for themselves first. So, they have children and in the beginning it all seems o.k.

"Look at these precious children I have. I love them so much and of course, look, they love me." And I hear Mothers, especially, saying, "They are my whole life, I would die for my children. What about living for your children and self-first? Because then there is diaper changing, feeding, taking care of them.

And as they grow up there are so many responsibilities, that we spend time waiting for them to grow into a different age thinking that it will be easier. And we spend our time being stressed and feeling like a failure.

And for some parents they just give up providing the two aspects of good parenting: boundaries, and unconditional love, especially for teenagers. They finally realize that their children aren't giving them what they thought they wanted, that inner peace and love they so desire.

And this is all because they don't take time to take care of themselves. I teach parenting courses and I remember at one workshop toward the end a woman stood and said she was so happy to find out that she wasn't the only parent who doubted themselves and several others agreed.

So, apparently having children isn't enough, in and of itself. And with those relationships, with spouse, children, friends, bosses, money, etc. people end up sacrificing themselves for some expectation that never comes. This is called the "Wheel of Sacrifice," This a tool to use to change those habits.

On the wheel, start at 12 with sacrifice. That is defined as doing something for others that you don't want to. Mostly we like helping others, but sometimes we don't. And then we sacrifice, go to 3 on the clock, which is expectation. We expect that person to like us better or do something in return. And when they don't, go to 6, we get angry. Then we feel bad about our anger, go to 9, we experience guilt. We shouldn't have gotten angry, so we then go to sacrifice. We don't want to feel guilty, it's a useless emotion, so we sacrifice and start all over again.

Do you see yourself on this wheel? Which aspect do we change to get off the wheel? (Look for the answer at the end of this lesson) The reason none of these situations feels complete in helping one feel enough within themselves, is that we don't feel complete within ourselves to begin with.

If we don't feel complete within ourselves, how can anything we get involved with help us feel complete? And if we don't feel whole and complete within ourselves, if we don't feel that we are enough, then we most likely don't feel that God is enough.

And without feeling whole and complete then we look to drugs legal and illegal. We look to alcohol and other stimulants to help us feel better. But they only do that for a short time, and they must take more and then more. We are not experiencing the deep love and joy we are told we deserve.

We have heard that statement from the Bible: "Seek ye first the kingdom of God within, and all things will be given unto thee." That means that we need to go within for the answers, that all we want we can have. But only by going within to God first, by stopping our separation from our Source, God, and Love.

Jesus said: "The Father and I are ONE." Not separate, but One. Therefore, everything that God is, is what we are. We have the two commandments also: 1) "Love the Lord thy God, with all of thy Heart and all of thy Soul." And if God is within us, then we need to love ourselves with all our heart and soul. 2) "Love they Neighbor as Thyself." Not more than or less than, but the same. SO, Is God Enough?

Let's look more at what God is. God is Love and we have heard about Love from God. How Love heals everything. And that Love is all there is, that is real. God is Good and we all deserve the good that awaits us here. God is everything within us and everyone.

God is Joy, Peace, Happiness, Abundance and Prosperity, as well as Balance, Health and Well-being and so much more. If you had those qualities within yourself, would you not feel enough? So then according to this truth we need to go inside to experience those God qualities, not look for them outside of ourselves.

To end, let me share with you some Essence Affirmations about Self-love from the 21-day Self-love program that I have.

- I have unconditional self-love and self-worth because God created me!
- I am blessed as a Son and Daughter of God!
- Be still and know that I AM God!
- I am made in the image of God, so of course I AM worthy and loveable!
- I AM God and fully know it, and fully deserving of unconditional self-love and worth!
- I AM, in truth, the Christ, the Buddha, the Eternal Self, so of course I have unconditional self-love and self-worth!
- I am literally an incarnation of God, and even though I make occasional mistakes, that does not affect my inherent unconditional self-love and worth!

Today is the day to see that you are enough because God in you is enough. "Be Blessed and walk in the knowledge and assurance that GOD is about to turn something around in your life."

The answer to Wheel of Sacrifice is guilt. That is a useless emotion and only leads to sacrifice. We feel guilty about everything regarding who-we-are. We apologize for who-we-are and ask for permission to BE who-we-are or what-we-want.

Namaste, I Love You and You are Loved

# Fellowship of Spirit
# 11/15/15
# Lesson 6
# YOU ARE LOVE

*The waves bow down before you.*

In this moment, I give all glory to God!! I believe God wants you to know that your agenda for this day has been set in your soul. The only question now is whether you will listen to that. Do you know why you are alive in the body that you have? To give voice, action, and physicality to God.

Therefore, every bone and muscle, every tendon and nerve, every organ of your body is the expression of Life seeking to know itself. Every cell resonates in harmony with the Divine Ideas of your health, prosperity and especially LOVE.

You need to know that everything necessary for the full and complete expression of vitality and wellbeing is yours. Why might you ask? For you to become the grandest version of the greatest vision you have ever held about Who You Are. Everything else is beside the point.

Those outside things will involve you, of course. They will grab you and hold you and make you think it is important today, but it will all be very much beside the point. Stay on course Beloveds. Stay on the course of Love.

We are here as I have talked about so often to connect to our soul, our I AM Consciousness, as that is the truth of who we are. As a result, for today, Spirit has given me a few different sharing's about Love and the soul.

#1- As it said in the previous statement, you are here to give voice and physicality to God. That means you need to know that you are love, Divine Love. In the ego mind, you think you are something else. You think you are less. Now, I understand that you do not always hold awareness of love in your heart. I understand you hold awareness of less than love, such as upset, anger, blame, attack, judgment, disturbance, outrage, despair, dislike and so much more, all FEAR. Because of these varied emotions, they make you think you are not love. Nevertheless, God has made you love.

God made you love from Its love. So, therefore, Love is who you are. Because Love is in a class of its own, you are in a class of your own. Those 'small' emotions are small stuff, even though they feel big. Once we give attention to them, we move into the past and they stop being small. And they grow in energy and take over your attention and connection to God. So, do not make them big. You know the old statement "Don't make a mountain out of a molehill." Making yourself live with a sense of smallness does not benefit you. Truthfully, what are these emotions that seemingly disrupt your love?

They are little bumps on our path of love that if ignored become bigger quickly. They create pain in our bodies that we put up with because they are so familiar to us. The lesser emotions may cover up your love. They take your attention away from love, and yet they cannot take your love away.

Why? Your love is established. It is permanent. God gave it to you. It is built in you. Your essence is love. Despite appearances, you are nothing but love. That is why I call them FEAR emotions, the lessor ones, as Love is more powerful. On the other side, the lesser emotions are here today and gone tomorrow. But Love is always waiting for you to let it emerge. Love is always there quietly waiting for you to wake up to that which you are made of. Love reigns.

Anything less than Love amounts to little bee stings. They don't belong there, and so they get out. They amount to nothing. But you are more. WHY? Because Love is everything. You are everything.

#2 - As humans, you confuse your body with yourself. That is because you live in them every day. Bodies are lessor 3-D instruments with daily functions. They hold all the pain we experienced in childhood and are instruments of communication, if only we paid attention to the pain. All the while, you are a Holy being, meaning you are total and undeniable LOVE.

Your love does not waver. Your love does not malfunction. Anything but love is nonsense. Anything but love makes no sense at all. Anything but LOVE is not real. It makes no sense to harbor anything but love. People go to a lot of trouble to dissuade themselves from love. They hurt people's feelings, and they hurt bodies. Some even go to the trouble of declaring war, killing other bodies. To what avail? The soul is eternal, the body is temporary. There is something in themselves that they want to kill. And it is not love.

They misunderstand love and so denounce it within themselves and affix the blame on others for how they feel. If anyone disguises the love within himself, no one else bears the responsibility but the person himself or herself. If one allows his anger to boil up, he has hoarded that which does not belong to him. Therefore, we have so many school and other shootings. They are blocked in their infinite love; they feel fear in the form of anger at someone or the world and then take it out on others. No one must keep their anger. It is not your right. We keep it because we want to feel right.

Anger takes away your strength. As you feel this anger energy, it angers you more because of how it makes you feel inside and a part of you knows that it is not the truth. You don't have to keep it. You certainly don't have to fool yourself into thinking that you must keep that which hurts you as an emblem of your rightness.

We need to remember or know that we are never angry at what we think we are. It is always about the past, buried within our body. And until we do the work to feel and release these old toxins, they will continue to haunt us and carry the anger around. Ask yourself, what can be right about what hurts you and that you might wish to defray to others, so they will hurt as you hurt? Nothing other than your own old painful thoughts and emotions stored in the body, believing that somehow you have been hurt and its payback time.

It is time to know that you have choices, and there are choices you must make. The main one is to get help and not hold on to the toxins in the body. That help would include really "feeling" those emotions as you did originally in childhood and then release them. This is the work I have done on myself and provide for clients. If you continue to hold these emotions and thoughts inside it is a choice you have made. If you made that choice, you could make another choice and another and another. You can choose to get up and replace each negative emotions and thoughts with love.

You can get up in love. You must get up in love. Undo from your heart anything less and everything else is less. You are more. You are love. Now live it, Beloveds.

#3 - God has said: Welcome to a world of love. This love resides in you and everywhere. You each are a fountain of love which vibrates everywhere and resides in Heaven within.

Whatever you do with your love, it flows to Heaven on earth. When you think of casting love on the world, picture yourself in a position of being a fisherman casting your line of love out into the water watching it flow away to the world and then back to you. Now picture tossing your love up as high as you can. The higher you toss your love, the wider your love will reach in the whole universe. Further than the soil you cast your love on because it is now in the heavens. Further than you could walk on the land, and joyfully further than your eye can see.

Loving the world is more than loving the planet, Beloveds, as I have expressed here. Simply love, as that is who you are, and your love will spread out from you to everyone and everything in the world and cover it with the radiance of your love. So, do you choose to do that and be amazed?

Understand that your love is heat and picture the rays of your love emanating out from you full of warmth and light. The rays of your love go further and further until the whole Universe is warmed by your love. Can you visualize your love going out, and coming back to you?

It is the most natural thing in the world when you allow it. That is the clue Beloveds, since that is who you are. Your love is God's love, and it becomes mightier and stronger. It's like loving the world with your Love, every day is Valentine's Day, and you give it a bouquet of flowers or a box of candy.

Then it connects with and expresses God's unconditional Love which makes your expression enormous, a hundred times bigger. You may have asked many things of God over the years. Now ask God to add to the quantity of love that emanates from you. Have you ever asked for this before?

Now it is no longer a question of asking God for love or even begging for love to reach you. After the Practice of the Presence inside, it is now a deeper understanding of your love reaching far, reaching therefore to the whole world. Say: "God, may the whole world receive my love. even if I am only able to send a little shoot of love. I know you will magnify it for me. I know that when my love reaches You, dear God, it is purified in the light of Your love. And my love becomes huge and reaches everywhere. Even a little bit of my love looms large when you see it. So, God, May I always make it easy for You to see my love and to make it bright. For this, I thank you, and keep You lit in my heart."

#4 - So, Beloveds, picture your love now, how your love flows. How you have felt your love and released it out into the world that is waiting for your love. Picture how your love is received. Picture how the world lifts its head.

Picture the world's love rising to God. That is how powerful your LOVE is. Picture the world's love coming back to you as God's pure love entering your heart, so that the love you give, and give is ever new for you. It is time to picture your love as the Oneness with God and All.

Namaste, I Love You and You are Loved

# Namaste Center Talk
# 3/22/09
# Lesson 7
# 4 BODIES OF GOD

*The trees extend their arms to shield you from the heat.*

A sleeping mind cannot see what is right in front of it, and that is why it is so important that you stay awake with me. You are like a person dying of thirst, asleep in a boat floating in an enormous freshwater lake, which could stand for being in our human emotions.

Wake up and see where you are in order to cleanse the past. There is no need to deny yourself the life-giving water of God's Love, which is also yours to give. Let this be the day that you give up your search and accept what has always been yours.

You are only denying yourself, which, as you have already discovered, is completely in this moment, I Give All Glory to God. This is a Divine time and place as we are gathered here together as family. Let's start with a Spiritual Peacemaking lesson: "Seek to understand this day, that the Love of God is your only desire and always has been."

No matter where your mind and ego seem to lead you, this alone will satisfy your souls longing. You came from God, were created like God, which means that God alone is the home you seek. And since this alone is real, you need only open your eyes to receive Love everywhere. Okay, are we all awake now? At least the best we can be? "Art of Spiritual Peacemaking"- James Twyman

So, we are here to learn about the four bodies of God. What are they and how can we practice the presence of these bodies in our lives? We are aware, somewhat, of the spiritual body of God, and probably believe that that is the only one.

That certainly is an important one. But what happens to those of us who are lightworkers, spiritually connected. We tend to pay attention to that one only and forget the other three. And I'm talking about energetic bodies.

By doing so, we then forget or deny important parts of ourselves. As we move forward on this spiritual path, we talk a lot about our consciousness. Do we know what we mean by that term? Let me give you an idea. Consciousness is the single most important thing in your spiritual path.

It is the foundation of your path on which all other aspects of your spiritual path are built. It is the total order and structure of all your active and dormant content, of all things that have occurred in your life—all your experiences, all your understanding, and all your wisdom.

It is all the information and content you have gathered and how it is structured within you, how it is integrated and synthesized within, how you see yourself, and all your life through it and whether you are programming it into your consciousness, the higher or lower aspects of all these things.

And that is the most important point to know, whether we are programming and therefore living from the higher aspects or the lower aspects. That is the God, Spirit, Mighty I AM Presence Self or the ego self of fear. We do not see through our physical eyes; we see through our consciousness.

And we tend to project out on to others and especially onto God, our current level of consciousness. It is estimated about 70% of our spiritual path is self-inquiry or how to process our consciousness, and the actions taken from that inquiry. Most lightworkers focus on the spiritual, and therefore do not have a clue as to what consciousness is and/or how to develop and refine theirs. As I have said, there are so many levels of our consciousness that includes all things in our lives. But for today, let's look at the other 3 bodies of God besides the spiritual that is affected by this consciousness.

Those three are: the mental or psychological, the emotional, and the physical. Now those three, of course, fit with the 3-dimensional beings that we are and this 3-dimensional life we live in. Most Ministers talk about and focus on the spiritual aspect. And yet, most congregational members then go home and must deal with their relationships, their jobs, their worries, their fears, etc. And then tend to bring those aspects of their consciousness back to the church. Why? Back in the middle '70's, I spent 5 years studying in a Gurdjieff school.

Anyone hear of Gurdjieff? He was a great teacher who spent his whole life trying to find the reason as to why he was here. He finally found and studied with the school that Jesus studied with when he disappeared those number of years, the Essenes. When Gurdjieff got out of this school, he started his own program called "The Work," and it was 4th way school. This meant that he knew we all lived in one of three bodies, physical, mental, or emotional. His goal was to help people learn how to balance all three, the 4th way connected to God and become more of a Master in their lives. This was the beginning of my metaphysical life, and I experienced a lot of change in this school. And I have continued to go thru more experiences in this school called life. That is exactly where we are, in a school called the

Earth plane. The goal here is to learn how to balance ourselves and live and express through all 4 bodies of God.

You might be saying, God is not one of those 3 bodies. Consider if God is living through everything there is in this Universe, then God is living in our bodies, our emotions, our thoughts, and we need, as Spiritual Beings, to pass all the initiations of these 3 as well as the spiritual. As I mention the word initiations, I am referring to everything that happens to us in our lives, because they are learning lessons that we have brought to us through our consciousness. That means it is time to release the thought that says, "I am doing something wrong, or someone else is doing something wrong to me." Whatever we experience in our lives are learning lessons, plain and simple, because our path, our journey here on earth is to become the Ascended Masters that we inherently are. And that basically means we need to take responsibility for all of what is happening "out there" in our world.

"Out there," is all a reflection of what is going on "in here" in our consciousness. I am very aware that everyone has their own ideas or definitions of every word in the dictionary. And that is why we have problems in communication, because we assume that everyone understands what we are saying.

But they don't, they have their own understanding. So, some of you may have had a negative reaction when I said the word responsibility. A more positive definition of that word is not blame or duty, but the ability to respond. To BE present with the moment and responding from Love. Does that seem a little easier? OK. I have lain a little of the foundation.

So, let's go over some of these aspects of the 4 bodies. Beginning with the physical, we want to look at such things as: our diet, physical fitness, proper grounding, work/sleep balance, repairing the aura and cleansing the cells, holistic health, overcoming bad habits and addictions.

This would include embodying the Mighty I AM Presence and Christ in your physical body on earth. Your body is the temple of God. How are you treating it? I look at the number of weight-loss programs we have in this society. And do they work? Apparently not. What is that saying?

That we cannot accept our bodies, unless they look like what someone else tells us they should look like. This tells us that we do not pay enough attention to all the other aspects of having a Christed body, except for weight loss. What about the work/sleep balance and the stress that imbalance causes?

What about holistic Health, alternative care, listening to the wisdom of the body? And adding that information to what Western medicine experts say. So again, God gave us this body and it is our responsibility to take care of it, to treat it as if God were living in it, because He/She is.

Let's go to the emotional body: We want to look at such things, as how to properly deal with our emotions, how to be aware of when we are in fear, and how to move to love. It doesn't just happen in one jump. Then, knowing that all our thoughts and emotions come under either Love or Fear.

Therefore, being aware of what state we are living in. Being aware of when we are living in our emotional body, too connected with fear emotions, worry, blame, judgment, etc. Along with the emotions are our physical initiations, such as: Keeping your earth life organized, mastering the laws of manifestation, helping to revamp earth civilization, living an earthly physical legacy by helping to create a Christed/Ascended Master civilization of earth, mastering relationships. (Ah, there is a big one.)

As a Relationship Consultant, I know that we have two main aspects of life, Relationship and Communication. That is the work I do, helping people learn more about their relationship with self and others, how they communicate and how to balance them with their spiritual understanding.

With those two we need to look at all the relationships we have in our lives and what is the relationship we have with ourselves. Then, communication. It is said only 60% of our communication is verbal, the rest is non-verbal. What messages are we sending out thru the non-verbal?

Remember the look your father or mother gave that you knew meant something or was misinterpreted somehow. Then we have the mental/psychological area, which would be such things as: Constantly BEing aware of our thoughts and when we are projecting on others. Developing a flawless character, seeing that you cause your reality, and you are not an effect.

You are a Master, not a victim. To practice what you preach, walk your talk and be in integrity in all you do. Owning your own personal power and self- mastery at all times. Developing the soul qualities needed to become the Mighty I AM Presence on earth, which is your deeper, individual connection to Spirit.

Refining your consciousness and developing the God/Christ/Spirit/Love self within. Knowing how your ego works. And

For instance, you might say I want to have more peace. Then I tell them they need to choose inside to BE more peaceful. It's the same with anything—you need to BE that first to eventually have what you want. Now, you ask, what about the Doing. That is God's job.

We have so many statements about God BEING our Source. Ask and you shall receive and many more. The process now is BE-DO-HAVE. You BE the person you want to BE regarding what you want and let God take care of the Doing, which might be telling you a step to take, but it is still from God. And then open your arms and accept your want.

BEING is composed of wisdom, will and consciousness. It takes all of these to make what we call God. Ideas exist eternally in wisdom; they are made manifest through will and that manifestation is called consciousness.

The man BEING the faculty of will in the Supreme Godhead and it is through him that the Universe is brought into manifestation. That which is brought forth is consciousness, a thing made. Passover: Represents the feeling of the spiritual man from the dominion of sense.

It is all part of the regenerative process that goes on in the body under the inspiration of the Christ mind. It is the passing over or out of one state of consciousness into another.

BEING-existence, the substance of essence of an existing person or thing.

As an example, I introduce myself after my name as: I AM a strong BEING of Love. Now I know that not all of you, about two-thirds, will connect with what I AM saying while another one-third will be questioning and asking: What is he talking about? He is being arrogant. And that is all o.k.

By my BEING who I AM gives others the freedom to claim theirs as well. The truth is we are all beings of Love, but we have forgotten that truth. The Bible says that God gave us the top two commandments. 1) Love the Lord they God with all thy heart mind and souls 2) And to love thy neighbor as thy self.

The key word here is Love, BE the BEING of Love. As non-physical beings, that is all we were, Light beings of Love. And then we came into human form as Human (GodMan) "Beings", but we began to forget our deeper truth.

We learned somewhere, along the way, from family, church, etc., that we needed to DO first, so we could have what we wanted and then we would be happy. DO HAVE BE. But we have had it all backwards. WE need to start BEING first, so then we can DO with God's guidance, the action steps of BEING.

And then we are open to the bounty of the Universe and start receiving all of that which we not only want but deserve as the powerful wonderful manifestations of God we are. Let's look at this a little bit. We were beings of light and love, still inherently within us.

We came into physical form and then began to forget the truth and went into fear. And, instead of claiming our divinity we believed that we had to do something to prove to the world that we were o.k. and that we deserved what we wanted.

As children, we played "AS IF" all the time, we moved in-between imaginations and physical results, we were fully and completely connected. Then we were taught as we grew up to only believe in what we could see or prove in actual "Physical world," to mistrust our imagination part of our experience.

We were taught to do, always be in action steps. And if we did enough, then we will have what we want, accepted, and loved. So, let's look at TAB - "Take Action Being." Just BE" who we are, just "BE" who we want to be, just "BE" the person of love.

Once we give ourselves permission to just BE, we then have made a connection with the Universe/God and then we will receive. When we take the action of opening ourselves up, we will then have the abundance of love we want.

Namaste, I Love You and You are Loved

# Hillside Community Talk
# 03-15-07
# Lesson 8
# BEING THE SOLUTION

*The trees lay their leaves before you on the ground.*

In this moment, I Give All Glory to God. "Dear God, May I be pregnant with the expression of a new BEING. Someone more magnificent than I have been; more powerful than I have been; healthier than I have been; more alive than I have been; more at cause than I have been; more tender than I have been; more compassionate and merciful than I have been; more full of love than I have been; more tolerant and less judgmental than I have been; more at one with myself and others; closer to You, dear Lord, than I have been. Amen."

How often, have you said a prayer like that one, most likely in a state of despair, hoping that it would bring about some change in your life? I know I have.

The clue word in that whole prayer is the word BEING. "May I be pregnant with the expression of a new being!!!!" What a powerful line that is. To be pregnant, meaning to be full of my BEING. To express this new BEING, which comes from inside, about who we are.

And that is the solution to every problem we have, who we are BEING!!! Not the DOING. That's God's responsibility. A few months ago, I was pleased to be here, and I gave a talk entitled "Human "Being." I described what those two words mean and how you could merge the 2 qualities together to become the wonderful, powerful, loving human beings that you all are.

Today, I want to take that theme further and help you see that the solution to all your problems is……. Who you are BEING!!

I had a picture in my mind in the beginning of what I wanted to talk to you about, but around Easter it changed somewhat. Which happens quite often as God gives me other ideas. It sort of reminds me of the little boy who was watching his father, a pastor, write a sermon. "How do you know what to say?" He asked. "Why, God tells me" said the father. "Oh, then why do you keep crossing things out?"

To begin, I want to talk to you about what an important and auspicious month MARCH was for getting in touch with our BEING. During that month, we had these important holidays. The "Ides of March," St Patrick's Day, beginning of Spring and Aries, Passover, and Easter. And the most important date, at least to me, my birthday, March 28th, which happened to fall on Passover this year.

What a month of celebrations and opportunities. And I want to explain to you the metaphysical/spiritual viewpoint of all those dates. Let's begin with the Ides of March.

That is just a term given to the middle of the month, which happens to be the 15th for March, May, July, and Oct. And the 13th for the rest of the year. What we really know about that date is the assassination of Caesar.

Caesar was Ancient Rome's greatest General and Statesman, and he single-handedly made Rome the center of an empire that stretched across Europe. He had a lot of power, but that power (defined in the dictionary as physical strength or control) was expressed outwardly in control of land, government.

This power frightened many of his opponents, who at one time had been men who had accepted many of his favors. But as is the case with this kind of power, their fears came up. What they had received outwardly from themselves could also be taken away.

Who were these men BEING? People who were experiencing LOVE or FEAR? They were individuals who felt controlled by someone or something OUTSIDE of themselves, therefore actually they were weak and in fear. And because of this fear of being controlled, they banded together and assassinated him.

What else can people in this situation do to gain their power back? Actually, the action steps of DOING that we become involved in as humans come from the state of BEING we are in, whether that is a state of weakness or power. Rather than the states of BEING of GOD.

Metaphysically, it was a time of letting go of external control and claiming more inner control, personal power, and love of our own inner BEING, which is God itself, if they were open to that. Rulership implies the joint activity of reason and will which means forcing all the faculties and powers to pay tribute in slavish carnal service to the mind and body—to the outer.

The truth is, that the inner man, as well as the outer, must be given proper attention and care. And it starts with the inner to be able to change the outer. Therefore, we have the statement, "Render unto Caesar what is Caesar's and render unto God what is God's."

This means that we must keep in harmony with the unenlightened human will until the spiritual grows strong enough, loving enough and wise enough in our consciousness to take its rightful dominion throughout our entire BEING.

So, the season starts with a message of going within, and giving power to that which is more real and lasting, the power of Source

Energy manifested inside, one's BEING of unconditional LOVE we call God. Every holiday has a metaphysical/spiritual meaning as God is in everything.

Next, we have St Patrick's B/D., March 17th. As a young man of 16, St Patrick was captured and sold as a slave in Ireland. During this time, he dedicated himself to Christianity (his religion within). After he escaped and went to his home in England, he became driven by the idea of converting the Irish people to Christianity.

Therefore, he studied and prepared himself. He then went to Ireland, started a mission, and eventually founded more than 300 churches and baptized more than 120,000 people. Contrary to what Caesar did in expressing his power to control people and gather land, St. Patrick felt a different calling.

He felt that he had an inner power, an inner message that God had called him to serve in this form. Patrick expressed his humility, gratitude, and thankfulness that God called him to serve the Irish. As a result, he became a success by allowing his BEING to guide him.

And we have the myths or legends of St. Patrick, as Jesus had his. We have heard how he charmed the snakes into the sea and used the shamrock to illustrate the idea of the Trinity.

Who was St. Patrick BEING to charm the snakes out? Historically, serpents and snakes represent fertility or a creative life force. As snakes shed their skin several times a year through sloughing, they are symbols of rebirth, transformation, immortality, and healing. Also, as a symbol of eternity and continual renewal of life. And water, or the sea, relates to cleansing, especially our emotions. All about BEING.

The shamrock, representing the trinity, relates to GOD, threefold in BEING, which usually relates to mind, idea, and expression; in other words, thought, word and deed. Ralph Waldo Emerson explained it as this: Thought is the Blossom, Language is the bud, and Action is the fruit behind It; the juiciness. So, we are all our own fruit trees.

Here, we are talking about the Trinity of GOD, which is mind, having the idea (of expressing himself into man), stating that idea (I create you in the image and likeness of myself), and then having man expressed. It is important to look at this also for us as humans.

How our thoughts and our words create our deeds, which tells us the power we have as co-creators. Another way to look at it is, the 3-foldness of man—Spirit, Soul, and Body. Spirit, a name for God, relates to (I AM), Spirit and Mind are synonymous; therefore, we know GOD/SPIRIT as Mind, the one Mind.

It is the Intelligence of the Universe. Soul relates to Consciousness (I AM CONSCIOUS).

Soul is man's consciousness, that which we have developed out of Spirit. Body relates to manifestation (I APPEAR). Therefore, Body, your body and my body, are the forms of expression of both spirit and soul.

And when man puts out of consciousness all his limitations and realizes the perfection of Spirit (GOD within), his body will be perfect. WOW, so we have moved from the outer of Caesar, the outer power to control, to the inner power of God BEING manifested in us in perfection.

It reminds me of a story about an important lesson in life regarding whom we are BEING, and what we receive when we do.

One night at 11:30 p.m., an older African American woman was standing on the side of an Alabama highway trying to endure a lashing rainstorm.

Her car had broken down and she desperately needed a ride. Soaking wet, she decided to flag down the next car. A young white man stopped to help her. Now, realize that this was generally unheard of in the conflict-filled 1960's. The man took her to safety, helped her get assistance and put her into a taxi.

She seemed to be in a big hurry but wrote down his address and thanked him. Seven days went by, and a knock came on the man's door. To his surprise, a giant console color TV was delivered to his home. A special note was attached. It read: "Thank you so much for assisting me on the highway the other night. The rain not only drenched my clothes, but also my spirits. Then you came along. Because of you, I was able to make it to my dying husband's bedside, just before he passed away. God bless you for helping me and unselfishly serving others" Sincerely, Mrs. Nat King Cole

So, Beloved's, you never know who you can affect in your life. And what can come to you when you are BEING who you are. And allowing GOD within to do the DOING.

Then we entered Spring and Aries time, astrologically. This is the time when nature awakens—flowers bloom, rebirth, coming out, warmth. And Aries is the Fire to make this happen, the youngest sign of the Zodiac, which again relates to rebirth, and its purpose is "I AM." This is the opportunity to allow our connection to the I AM of Spirit to be manifested from within to our outer world.

We can awaken to the inner truth that has been hibernating in us and now express our rulership from a place of personal power, which might include more will and power. Not just reason and will like Caesar.

Life that appears in spring symbolizes the new life gained by death of the old and resurrection of the new which leads us to Passover and Easter. Metaphysically, Passover represents the freeing of the spiritual man from the dominion of sense. It is part of the regenerative process that goes on in the body under the inspiration of the Christ mind. Therefore, we are "passing over" or out of one state of consciousness into another. We are "passing over" from the state of being asleep, hibernation.

Also, the state of expression of self from the rulership of reason and will (Caesar), into BEING—which is composed of wisdom, will, and consciousness of Soul, spirit, and body, the Expression of the Unity, and rebirth into the truth of who we are, "I AM THAT WHICH I AM."

Three days into the spring, we celebrated EASTER. This is a return to the life of Jesus the Christ, which also represents God's idea of man in expression, relating back to what I mentioned earlier about the trinity. To put on the new man, new BEING, to bring forth the Christ in ourselves, we MUST put away the old thought of error and limitation (back to Caesar), to the new.

To accomplish that is to accept the truth of our BEING in faith. And through this new understanding, to live TRUTH in thought, word, and deed. In other words, to live our BEING, which is a manifestation of the Mind of GOD, to accept this I AM truth and let it blossom forth (as the fruit), to be reborn into the manifestation of GOD.

As Ernest Holmes, founder of Science of Mind, said: "GOD, AS MAN, IN MAN, IS MAN." That is who we are, that is our BEING, that is our answer to every situation in our lives. How powerful this time of two weeks were in expressing the energies we had available to make this new choice.

And my birthday was right in the middle of it. So, I got to receive all that energy. I got to be re-born. I got to experience more of my BEING, who I am, which is George, meaning the farmer, or Sower of seeds.

A wonderful, powerful loving human BEING, whose mission is to wake up as many people to the power of Love. And that is who I am BEING and what I am expressing from my BEING every time I speak or facilitate a workshop or talk.

Let me pull this together, to wrap it all up. During this time, we have come more into BEING, which is the existence, the substance or essence of an existing person. It is the wisdom, will, and consciousness which makes up the term GOD, which we are made up of, God, in us, as us, is us.

It is the solution to all our problems. It is our true BEING. Therefore, any problems that you have, that come into your life, money, health, relationship, love, work, anything, know that the solution is: To look at who you are BEING in relationship to it and let GOD handle the DOING.

An ending thought for you, about who you are BEING. Quote "You're going to change the world today. Now, don't try to deny it. And you know, I understand that it can be a little overwhelming to have the entire world depending on you. But I know that YOU can do it. I knew you could do it when I first met you. When I first saw the hunger in your fingertips and the fire in your eyes. When you spoke in just that way; with those words, in just that rhythm, that said: 'I'm going to change the world, gonna make it a little better; a little sweeter; a bit truer.'"

And I remember the way you said that nothing on this or any other planet, was going to stop you. Then you turned and walked away, confident, and clear. And I remember thinking to myself that YOU were amazing, that I'd never met anyone quite like you, and I was sure that if you put your mind and hands to it, there was nothing that could break you.

SO, there you sit, knowing that today's the day. Because I see the way you're shifting nervously in your chair. The way your body crackles and zaps, the way your grin says that YOU'VE decided that there is no time like now to move. YOU'RE going to change the world TODAY. I'm just glad I was here to see it. GO out and BE the Power you are—The Universe

The BEING SOLUTION is expressed this way. Our society lives by this process: DO-HAVE-BE.

Meaning we are told that if we do something then we'll have what we want and then we will BE happy or peaceful, etc.

It starts in childhood when our parents tell us, not necessarily in words, to clean our rooms or study and get good grades in school and if we do, we'll BE loved or BE happy or they will be proud of you. That starts a lifelong belief that we must do something to BE happy, etc.

For instance, we understand that if we get a job, we'll have money and we'll BE Prosperous. If we find someone who loves us, then we'll BE loved. And so on. Does this work? No. Because we leave ourselves out, relying on other people or things outside of ourselves to make us happy which doesn't work.

So, the process needs to change. We need to put ourselves first in our lives, which is something we are never taught in childhood. We then concern ourselves about others' feelings instead of our own. Of course, you may not understand how to BE, so I ask my clients what they want to have, then they can choose the BE part to receive what they want.

NAMASTE, I Love You and You Are Loved

## Lesson 9
## BEING ALONE with the BELOVED

*The leaves are there for you to walk in softness.*

In this moment, I Give All Glory to God! As you are aware in my talks, I have explored the concept of BEING, not DOING. Since these talks are about connecting to God's Love, we may need to explore how to bring our divine partner to us. BEING can be difficult to comprehend and use at times.

People think it takes work to create that partnership, so they believe they must DO something rather than use the process in the last lesson, and that is turn it over to God. They don't think about connecting in the stillness and LOVE of their heart, their partners heart and God's heart, because we are all one in LOVE.

We might first ask who is the Beloved? That would be God first. Because God is the Creator of all, the BEINGNESS of LOVE in all of creation. The second Beloved is all of us, you and your partner and all couples as God is in them and the relationship.

How can we accomplish that? Know that BEING with your partner, is BEING with the Beloved GOD and to accomplish that union you must create your spiritual practice, to clear out fearful thoughts and negative emotions, so that you surrender your heart to GOD and the relationship.

And secondly, by BEING the person whom you need to BE, to deepen the connection in manifesting this wonderful divine relationship. I suppose many of you have never thought of that, who you need to BE for this relationship to survive and thrive. Most people put the responsibility on their mate.

This is important to know and practice because the divine relationship is about you and how you will come from your Christ self and see the Christ in your partner. You want to know that you are connected to the Beloved in the quietness and loneliness of the One heart.

How wonderful it is to understand and connect to this ONE Heart of Love. And as I mentioned earlier, we need to always "Practice the Presence." We need to know that it takes quiet time of meditation and listening to our deep desire, listening to our partner's desire, both of which is God's Will, the heart of God.

When we quiet our mind to listen to receive instead of projecting out to the relationship, something wonderful can happen. We need to take the time to really "Feel" what's going on with us. To take the time to sit down with the quietness we're experiencing which brings up a lot for us to consider.

We may have fears of relationship come up. And that is o.k. as we deeply feel them and release them. Our mind might also bring up thoughts around who the person should be or what you would like the relationship to be. But we need to stay open with the heart inside. And when we do, we may find something remarkable, something wonderful, and something even better than you may have imagined. Connecting to the One Heart, we discover that because relationships are for learning, we understand that our partner is always a reflection of your mind.

This is then our opportunity for learning, resolution and mastery in myself, and my partner. Therefore, I always work at love and acceptance rather than blame and attack. We find that there is magic in our partnership, if we just surrender to God, the One Heart, and the Love.

This is trust in GOD to allow the flow of this Divine Love deeper within our consciousness. It then becomes time to go of any fears, especially resistance to that wonderful state of LOVE.

It becomes time to connect to the Law of Attraction, knowing that you will attract a partner that matches your vibration of relationship.

It always happens as a Law of the Universe, and it can either be a match of fear or Love. The question is which would you prefer to create? The time we are connecting to quietness, we need get out of our mind, so we can KNOW what GOD knows, which is as I mentioned earlier, only the BELOVED.

And by taking the time to sit with the inner quietness we may feel more of the loneliness hiding beneath the LOVE. We then need to take the time to go deep and instead of finding ourselves wanting this relationship to fulfill us, we then need to feel the inner loneliness we have carried inside all our life.

We see how we have used relationship to block feeling the pain of our separation from our Source. We feel how we tried to cover it up or release it thru the other relationships we had in the past but realize we never could. And as a result, we carry a belief about being a failure.

This ultimately stops us from really connecting to the Beloved in the way we want. Therefore, we need to connect to the One Heart in the stillness we choose to go thru. By experiencing that deep pain we had hidden, we become just you, your partner, and the BELOVED, all ONE.

We then feel a willingness to just BE, allowing the connection to a deeper state of BEING in Oneness with the universe. When that happens, we feel patient, because we now know the higher truth, we no longer wait for the next relationship.

We are connected to the real Heart of the Beloved God and open for the Beloved of our partner. Because of the BEING work we have done with the Beloved inside, we discover that if we can't be alone with the Beloved, we cannot be present with another. We then want to hold the Beloved inside as we spend our days living our life.

WE now understand that it is that time we spent alone with the Beloved that makes us the partner that our partner has always been looking for. That is because you connected to your BEING as has your partner. And you let GOD take care of the DOING.

My time with the BELOVED has shown me that I AM here fully engaged as a spiritual being, to now serve mankind as an example. And that example is my mission, which is to wake up as many people as possible to the power of LOVE. And my Beloved joins with me in our One Heart.

This asks the question: Do you want to BE like the man in that story in Lesson One, afraid of love? Or like the child giving love unconditionally? DO you want to be in a place of need, wanting love from another human or being connected with the BELOVED inside? Loving yourself and loving GOD within you will give you all that you desire. The choice is yours.

Namaste, I Love You and You are Loved

# Fellowship Talk
# 4-21-13
# Lesson 10
# THE POWER OF COMMITMENT TO GOD

The wind sinks to a whisper around your holy head.

In this moment, I Give all Glory to God. A Blessing to start for this lesson: Practicing Spirituality with Jesus, "LIVE IN THE PRESENT." Only now do I begin to understand better what Jesus meant when he said, "The Kingdom of God is at hand." Jesus was telling us that we don't have to wait to go "there." That "there" can be "here." -- John Aurelio in "Returning's."

To practice Jesus today: "Live in this moment. Monitor your language for any signs that you are dwelling on what has happened to you in the past or thinking about what might happen to you in the future. Instead, speak in the present tense. Use the words, "I AM."

Here we are talking about a scary word for some, Commitment. There are a lot of words in our vocabulary that we have learned their fearful, negative aspects. It is time to start looking at these words in a more positive, spiritual sense. Then we get past the old fearful training we received and into balance of ourselves.

And therefore, I say to you, YOUR life can be better if you have a commitment to something, especially God. Those who have truly worked their way up to a better life have had a commitment of some sort, be it to oneself or to another. COMMITMENT helps to keep one FOCUSED until achieving the desired goal. When people are committed to something, they maximize their effort of time and energy. Maximizing one's effort increases the likelihood that results will be achieved.

Now, you could say that there have been many people who have been committed to achieving goals without a conscious thought about GOD. And that is true. Unconsciously, through commitment, they have drawn upon GOD'S Presence and Resources to achieve what they wished for.

You might ask, "if that is true, why even bother to consciously bring God, into the premise of the power of commitment?" The reasons are many and primary is: that what a person may be committed to might possibly not be what is in their best interest, though on the surface it might seem so.

Think about setting goals at the beginning of the year. Are they always in your best interest? How many are done for external reasons? And how many of them get completed? The ego can get us set up in numerous situations that don't benefit us.

Ultimately, at the center of life in the body, mind, heart, and soul of everyone is GOD'S PRESENCE as the Real Life of us all.

God created you and lives within you to give you physical life and consciousness. Your soul is on an eternal path or voyage, which means you have numerous lives to choose who you want to be. Your life is always about the journey to Love. Did you know that? The life you are living right now is a GIFT from GOD.

The outer you, the ego, had absolutely nothing to do with you being here. It is the innermost you of GOD'S Presence that has given you this lifetime to live. God is the ultimate Real Life of your Body, Mind, Heart, and Soul. God has a plan—a Divine Plan for you in this lifetime.

As you grow close to GOD within you, you will grow closer to that plan. Neglect GOD, or be totally unaware of GOD'S Presence, and one's personal ego will attempt to discern and establish what the goals are for this lifetime, and it will BE out of fear.

Commitment may thus be made to personal ego goals, which may be very distant from the plan that GOD might intend for you to live in this lifetime. The personal ego on the surface may have its moments of glory, while one's soul may remain desolate.

If, on the other hand, you make a commitment to GOD, then you bring forth more of God's divine attributes of wisdom, creativity, love, healing and will to give you greater power to achieve your goals. Best of all, the goals that you will be achieving are GOD'S GOALS for your life.

This means that real progress is being made by your soul's growth. Real Progress is the fulfilling of your Soul, that place where your soul feels it's state of fulfillment. Only when this is present, is there any real happiness? For this reason, many people who were committed to achieving goals, upon fruition found no lasting happiness.

Have you experienced that? Completing something and still not happy? Because we spend time thinking that by completing something we will finally feel happy. That is still looking out there. That is why there are so many outwardly successful people who turn to drugs, alcohol, and other ways of escape.

They try to mask or cover their emptiness that they still feel, despite their other accomplishments. It might be said, therefore, that all victories in life without GOD are shallow victories. These are greatly dulled by the heartache that the soul feels for its lack of fulfillment.

For this reason, commitment should first be made to GOD in your life. There are appropriate words from the bible to illustrate, i.e. "What profiteth a man if he gaineth the world and loseth his soul?"

Being committed to God is ULTILMATELY being COMMITTED to the real life of your Body, Heart, Mind and Soul, the 4 bodies of GOD. In the spiritual reality of Truth you are always ONE with all that is. You lose illusions and gain perspective. You are fortified and nourished by GOD'S SPIRIT and MIND within you. So, commit to that Soul within you, which is God's plan and be surprised as to the outcomes.

NAMASTE, I Love You and You are Loved

# Namaste Center Talk
# 5/19/09
# Lesson 11
# WHAT DOES GOD SEE?

*All living things are still before you.*

In this moment, I Give All Glory to God. We'll discover in this lesson these tools as a way of commitment to God.

Body. Your body is a vehicle through which your mind, heart, and soul seek to fulfill themselves.

Your body could be thought of as a divinely ordained instrument through which God's will for your Soul can be accomplished on this physical plane of existence. It is therefore considered a physical manifestation of SPIRIT. God is living though you in your body.

Every movement or action you take is Spirit working through it. Every bone and muscle, every tendon and nerve, every organ of your body is the expression of Life seeking to know Itself. Every cell resonates in harmony with the Divine idea of Source.

The bible states this; "Know ye not that you are the temple of the living GOD?" The body houses SPIRIT, and when the mind, heart, and soul are committed to SPIRIT, the body seeks to do the will of GOD in this lifetime. Committing your body to GOD is committing your BODY to be used in the service of GOD for the will of GOD.

This does not mean that you must live in a monastery, or as the fakirs of India do, laying on bed of nails, to give the pain to GOD. The body can still express in earthly ways, such as sports, lovemaking, and the like, if you balance them out.

It is simply that the ULTIMATE use of the body and its energy is to be used to fulfill GODS WILL for your life in terms of accomplishment (BEING). Be it commerce, creative arts, sports, entertainment, healing, or spirituality. That is why it is important to be aware of the thoughts you put into your body, because you are talking about GOD.

If there is some issue with the body, it is time to get a spiritual answer and go to GOD. "There is a Spiritual Answer to Every Problem"—Wayne Dyer. When one's body energy is spent in commitment to GOD, it will feed one's soul.

Committing the energy of your BODY to the WILL of GOD harnesses the POWER of GOD to maintain, restore and regenerate your body throughout your life. The Body is also the body of communication, telling us through pain any disorder it's experiencing or toxins we have stored in it. AFFIRMATION: I COMMIT MY BODY to GOD in this life and thorough eternity.

Mind. Your mind exists on many different levels, from the conscious human level to unconscious memory levels, to the collective unconscious levels, to other dimensional levels and to the SOURCE of all levels—the GOD level at the center of your mind.

SPIRITUALLY, the word "commitment" when used in relation to GOD, means COMMITMENT at ALL levels of your mind to do GOD'S will for your life. To be willing to follow your inner intuitive divine guidance from GOD as to what to do with your life.

When you commit your mind, i.e. the human level and all other levels, a wonderful thing happens; you increasingly become under the influence of GOD'S mind. And what does GOD'S MIND carry? Thoughts of Fear or Thoughts of Love?

The power of GOD'S mind flows through your conscious mind, producing greater creativity, will, focus, determination, clarity of mind, and divine purpose to your goals, regeneration, healing, intuitive guidance, and unseen support. This means that various psychic energies are activated to cause effects to benefit you on the physical plane of existence.

Certain people may be drawn to you and you to them that will benefit everyone concerned. When you commit your mind on all levels, you are also in tune with such levels where GOD gives you the unseen support of which I speak. Thus, the more of your mind that is committed to God, the more freely consciousness flows in unseen realms to support you.

Your conscious mental attitude should be one of dedicating your mind completely to GOD, which does not mean retreating from physical life. On the contrary, when your mind is more committed to GOD, your presence will be a blessing to others, because you are Practicing the Presence of God.

This will harness Gods power by channeling GOD'S Divine Attributes into your physical life activities. Affirmation: "I COMMIT My Mind at all levels to GOD in this lifetime and through eternity."

Heart: What does God see? Only the Beloved. What does God feel? Only Love. The truth is, all there is, is Love, the rest we made up. When you commit your Heart to the Heart of GOD, then you are feeling, experiencing and BEING the LOVE that GOD is. That is pure love, unconditional love, Higher Love.

We work at understanding Love through our mind, but our mind cannot realize LOVE as powerful as LOVE is. The only way to experience it through our mind is to commit our mind to GOD, as I just mentioned. To experience our HEART is not DOING, Thinking, or action of any kind. It is just BEING.

We have the physical heart that beats within our body that keeps us alive. We use this organ as a symbol of LOVE. And yet, we have so many fearful statements that we use "You broke my heart, my heart is closed. My heart is open to you, I don't love you, I only like you. Don't take my heart away, my heart is in pain." and on and on.

Do those statements sound like the statements of GOD? DO they sound like the statements of LOVE? We might want to investigate the idea of our heart even deeper. And acknowledge the sacred heart that is right next to the physical heart. But why limit it there?

Do you think that God would limit its love to just a certain part? Why not go further and say that Love is within ALL of your Body, Mind and Soul. To know that there is no place that LOVE is not. Love is our heart, our body, the air we breathe, the house we live in, the car we drive.

The person sitting next to you, the eyes that you look into. Just consider for a moment, the power of this LOVE. LOVE so strong that God desired to create aspects of itself. So, there were more to experience this love. LOVE so strong, that all there is, is Love, acceptance, non-judgment.

We have been told that, it is impossible to understand and realize the Love of GOD. I tell you now that this should be our only goal. For what can this love be but an extension of the peace that surpasses the world of separation and form?

We feel separate, not only from each other, but from ourselves, from our body, from our heart, from everything especially from GOD. And yet, in God's mind, and heart there is no separation. There is no form. There is only ONE, there is only Itself, recreated. And all it is, is LOVE. Nothing else. For us it is impossible to realize the LOVE of GOD if you cling to conflict of ANY kind. The Love of GOD can only be found in the world where you really live. The home that you have never left. Affirmation: "I commit my Heart to the only Truth there is, the LOVE of GOD"

Soul. There is a part of your mind that lives on through eternity. Within its energies are the memories of past lives and the promises of lives yet to be. It is that part of you—the closeness of God—that is sacred. It is the most valuable part of you, because IT IS ......YOU!

When you commit your soul to God, you commit the very essence of Who and What you really are to GOD. When you do this on a spiritual level, your mind is purified with GOD's Light. Indeed, it is sacred. Because it is sacred, it produces a flow of GOD's Love into your consciousness.

This makes you more compassionate and understanding of others. By having the traits of compassion and understanding, your power among others is increased because they respond and love you. The power of Love is therefore more present in your life.

Yes, Love is POWER, for there is no greater Power than Love to motivate a person to great heights and accomplishments. IF your Soul is committed to GOD, there is the inner joy and happiness that comes from increased INNER ONENESS with God's Presence.

Affirmation: "I COMMIT my SOUL to GOD in this life and thought eternity." Because a person engages in spiritual studies and practices does not guarantee a better, more fulfilled life. There are many people who are filled with spiritual knowledge, intellectually, but have missed the mark spiritually.

They can quote you lesson and verse, but their lives don't represent those beliefs. And others are mystical intellectuals. They express the mysteries of life but are light years away from truly connecting with GOD's Presence. What is missing is the real commitment of their Body, Mind, Heart, and Soul to GOD.

SO, Beloved's, it is time to enter your heart of hearts, where GOD knows your innermost thoughts and genuinely commit your Body, Mind, Heart, and Soul to GOD. The years and lifetimes to follow will prove to you the wisdom of your commitment.

Prayer treatment: DIVINE MIND, MY CREATOR, whose Spirit and Light live within me, I affirm and declare the total Commitment of my Body, Mind and Soul to your Presence and by your grace and Love my life through eternity is blessed, for this I give thanks. I let it be so… and so it is!

So, Beloved's, use this day to Practice the Presence, Commit to God through your mind, Heart, Body and Soul, and BE amazed at what happens.

NAMASTE, I Love You and You are Loved

## Fellowship Talk
## 5-19-13
## Lesson-12
## RAISING YOUR VIBRATIONAL RATE

*All living things are still as they recognize who walks with you.*

In this moment, I give all glory to GOD. Good morning Beloved Beings, and welcome to this place of Love. Every place we are is always a place of Love and all we need do is be open to it. Every place we stand is a Holy Place and every moment of time is a Holy Moment.

I usually give a joke to end my service, but here is one in the beginning to coincide with the lesson. oly nstant,

There were these 3 salesmen. One was Hindu, one was Jewish, and the other was… a… complainer. So, they had been working together during the day, the 2 putting up with the complaints of the other.

They really didn't like being around him because he complained so much. The day was over, and they were traveling out of town to the next city. It was getting dark, and they had no idea where they were, but they found a farmhouse to make a stop. They asked for rooms to spend the night. The owner told them that he had 2 rooms for them, but the 3rd one would have to spend the night in the barn. So, the Hindu said, "I will do that, you two take the bedrooms."

Sometime later in the morning, there was a knock at the door. Since the other 2 bedrooms were right by the door, the 2 salesmen got up and answered. It was the Hindu man. He said "Listen, there is a cow in there, and they are very special animals to our faith. I cannot spend the night there." "Okay," the Jewish fellow said, "come in I will go to the barn." So, he did, and everyone went back to bed. Later, there was another knock at the door. The 2 salesmen answered it and it was the Jewish person, "There is a pig in the barn, and they are not animals we acknowledge. So, I cannot spend the night in the barn."

"Okay," the complainer said, kind of upset: "That only leaves me, I guess I'll have to spend the night there. They all went to bed. Sometime later, there was another knock at the door and the 2 salesmen went to the door. And it was the cow and the pig standing there.

I share that because it fits in with the talk for today, Practicing the Presence. First, I want to share a heartfelt blessing: "The word 'appreciation' means to be thankful and express admiration, approval, or gratitude. It also means to grow or appreciate."

"As you appreciate life, you become more valuable—both to yourself and others."—Sara Paddington, author of "Hidden Power of the Heart." As we learn how to appreciate those experiences that we don't like, as much as those we do like, life becomes more joyful, and we become freer. You might think of it as a good trade-off. That is a blessing that we will incorporate into today's talk. My first time here to speak at this church was last September 23rd and I talked about Practicing the Presence. I am going to expand on that today by bringing in information about Vibration and how to raise it.

In the beginning, the Creator wanted to share itself (or himself, for those used to that gender term) and all its powerful, positive aspects. So, it created itself in the Universe, through the planets, the animals, water, plants, and all other species. This also includes souls that became humans.

In this non-physical form, we were totally connected to Unconditional Love. Our thoughts were powerful, as they are now. And we were able to create anything we desired, just as our Creator could. We were created in the image and likeness meaning that we were Unconditional Love.

We were Prosperity; we were Health; we were everything, especially LOVE. Not only were we created in its image, but also God/Spirit was alive in us. We were ONE, there was no separation. Everything in the Universe was and still is energy/vibration.

This means, all things were created out of energy, the core of the cells vibrating at a high or low level. The planets and all other life forms, have cells at their core consisting of energy, as that is what God is. So here we were light bodies, souls, vibrating at a high level of energy.

We were and are One with God, creating all we wanted through our thoughts. We then chose to come into physical body on this planet, to use it as a school, to forget the truth of who we were so that we could have experiences, and learning lessons, to re-learn again the truth of who we are.

That, of course, is Unconditional Love. And the most important reason was to be in this body so that God could experience through us in this form. God fulfills Itself as our individual Being, meaning God is in us, as us, is us. God experiences us as our/It's BEING, our/It's Soul, our/It's Mighty I AM Presence.

We talk about creating Heaven on Earth. And it is possible, but that happens only to the degree in which we let God fulfill Itself as our individual experience. God is the Universal mind or Intelligence, expressing in everything within the Universe. And God is also the individual mind or intelligence.

It is our inner Selfhood, God, which appears outwardly as you or as me. I AM…is the Lord; I AM…is the God; I AM…is the Creator.

Namaste, I Love You and You are Loved

# Hillside Center
## 8-15-07
## Lesson 13
## PRACTICING THE PRESENCE

*The Light you carry is also those who see you.*

In this moment, I Give all GLORY TO God! As Joel Goldsmith says in his book, "Practicing the Presence:" "This is not the personal sense of selfhood, which walks the earth calling itself Bill, Mary or Henry, saying arrogantly, "I am God." No, it is a gentle whisper in the ear that says: "know ye not; I AM in thee and thou in Me. We are One in the midst of the Almighty."

Well, that is put in the form of Bible language, but it says: "This I, which is God, has made us in Its own image and likeness, and have given us Its nature and Its character." There is a power governing us, caring for us, protecting us, maintaining us, and sustaining us. I have an affirmation that I say daily, "The Universe loves me, supports me and nourishes me and wants me to win." This power is the conscious remembrance of the I, the infinite nature of individual being which must be continuously practiced.

Fulfillment comes about only as you and I can relinquish the personal sense of self in order that God may fulfill itself. Spiritual fulfillment means God fulfilling Itself, fulfilling Its Destiny. Our job then: to let God BE the only Presence; the only power; let God BE the Light and let it all shine thru us.

So, the next question might well be, "How do we do that? First of all, by Practicing this Presence. That title means that we are working at it; we are working at remembering, we are working at waking up from the sleep of the ego. As children we still remembered our truth. We stuffed this big light body into this little human body. We were born, and we still knew the truth. That is why we see so much innocence in babies, because the Light and Unconditional Love is still expressing itself. That is why children are so fidgety, as we call them, because they are getting used to this little body that they are in.

the next thing that happens is that they begin to forget this truth about themselves. Oh, not at first. You say anything to a child that is the opposite of their truth, and they will disagree with that because they know. As Marianne Williamson writes in her book, A RETURN TO LOVE. "When we were born, we were programmed perfectly. We had a natural tendency to focus on love. Our imaginations were creative and flourishing and we knew how to use them. We were connected to a world much richer than the one we connect to now, a world full of enchantment and a sense of the miraculous." Do you all remember that about yourself as a child?

Namaste, I Love You and You are Loved

# Fellowship Talk
# 3-23-17
# Lesson 14
# EVERYTHING IS ENERGY

*All things alive see in you, their holiness.*

In this moment, I Give all Glory to GOD. Here are some principles of Energy to consider. The basic component of everything in the Universe is made of energy, from the biggest planet to the smallest rock. This includes our bodies, our cells, blood, thoughts, and words.

Overall, the human energy system is a finely balanced, independent system. Every thought we think is psychic energy and attracts its' like on a psychic level. Every word we speak is vibrational energy, filling the immediate atmosphere with an unseen, but very real psychic vibrational energy, attracting to us the likeness of our thoughts and words.

Energy vibrates at different rates of speed, and thus has different qualities. Therefore, positive thoughts and words have a high vibrational rate, and negative fearful thoughts and words have a low vibrational rate. When we have blocks of energy, we need to get energy moving in that area.

We have the physical body of communication, mental body of creation, the emotional body of feelings and attraction. These relate to the emotional healing work I do to clear out the body for God's Love to BE felt. Keys to removing a block are: Mental, emotional, and physical acceptance, relaxation, and release.

Also, clear observation which leads to understanding of the root of the problem and being able to feel it and let go of it. This root is not Spiritual; that is, we are not connected to Spirit within us when we have problems. Remember, in the Practicing the Presence of God, there is only God in everything.

Another step is gratitude, as I mentioned in the beginning. Being grateful for everything you have, for life. INNONENCE IS PRICELESS. One Sunday morning the pastor noticed little Alex standing in the foyer of the church staring up at a large plaque. It was covered with names with small American flags mounted on either side of it.

The seven-year-old had been staring at the plaque for some time. So, the pastor walked up, stood beside the little boy and said quietly, "Good morning, Alex." "Good morning, Pastor," he replied, still focused on the plaque. "Pastor, what is this?" he asked?

The pastor said, "Well, son, it's a memorial to all the young men and women who died in the service." Soberly, they just stood together, staring at the large plaque. Finally, little Alex's voice, barely audible and trembling with fear, asked: "Which service, the 9:15 or the 11:15?

We have 5 bodies of health: physical, mental, emotional, social, and spiritual and if one part of the system is unbalanced, it distorts the whole system. Developing the spiritual body is impossible if the spiritual body is obstructed. A childhood hurt held and retained in one's energy blocks perceptions, understanding, and skews spiritual development.

So, what happened? Why is it that we reached a certain age, looked around and the enchantment was gone? Because we were taught to focus elsewhere. We were taught to look at a world that contradicts who we are. And our job is to work on going back and looking at the truth within us. Our job is to reconnect with the vibrational energy of Unconditional Love, Innocence, Joy and Happiness, as well as all the other qualities of Spirit within us. We can only create according to the mental equivalent of your consciousness. Your mental atmosphere speaks to the Consciousness of God and brings to you all you receive.

Let's do a little visualization. Close your eyes and visualize the highest vision of yourself that you can. Whatever you can imagine that your life looks and feels like, or your relationships, whatever you desire. Now hold on to it and listen to GOD'S voice saying:

I AM ALL THINGS IN YOU. 3-4 times Come back, know that Everyone is here on earth but for one purpose, and that purpose is to show forth the glory of God, the divinity and the fullness of God, and especially to LOVE. Are you ready to do that? How are you going to do that? By raising your Vibration.

Again, you and God are One. Show your light through your thoughts, your words, your actions, your gratitude, your understanding of your purpose here. You're Practicing the Presence of God within every moment of the day. So, BE Awake, have a Blessed Day.

Know that God wants you to know that the yearning for love in your life is about to end in the most wonderful way. It is impossible to yearn for that which you already have, and you are about to see and realize that all the love you could ever want is coming to you now.

Open your heart and you will see it right in front of you. I am glad that you read this today. And so is God.

NAMASTE, I Love You and You are Loved

# Fellowship Talk
# 3-23-18
# Lesson 15
# AWAKENED HEART

*Seeing their holiness, they salute you as savior and GOD.*

In this moment, I Give All Glory to God! I have talked to you about resurrection before and this seems the opportunity to explain that term more. Resurrection is a term used mostly at Easter about the Jesus' experience after the crucifixion.

It is a vibrational energy situation which is the raising of man's mind and body from physical sense or the 3-D world to one's spiritual consciousness, like what I said about Ascension. This is accomplished by the quickening action of the Holy Spirit. Then we ask what is the Holy Spirit?

I am sure you have heard the terms Father, Son, and Holy Spirit. Growing up Catholic I heard and used those words a lot. It is a term to describe the Source of all manifestation which is in the mind, the body of creation. Which is exactly like the Father, our Creator, to a degree.

Though we did not create all that God has, we created only from our mind and in our own world. An idea arises in a man's mind of something that he wants to do or have. This idea is the Son, as the Son of the Father. Then man expresses that idea in definite thought which is the Spirit going forth to accomplish that desire where he has been sent.

The Father is the beginning principle. The Son is that Principle revealed in a creative plan and the Holy Spirit is the executive power of both Father and Son carrying out the creative plan. Father is the Absolute Being; Son is the I AM identity of the BEING, and the Holy Spirit is the form and personality of the BEING.

As Science of Mind says, this is the true nature of the ONE GOD, Spirit, Soul, and Body: Father, Son and Holy Spirit/Holy Ghost. So, back to the earlier statement, the raising of man's mind from sense to spiritual consciousness is accomplished by the Holy Spirit, the executive carrying out the plan.

I am going to say some bible phrases here, so bear with me as I explain. Romans says: "If the Spirit of him that raised up Jesus from the dead dwelleth in you, then he shall give life also to your mortal bodies through his Spirit that dwelleth in you." "The resurrection is not for the soul alone."

"I AM the resurrection and the life." Jesus is quoted. "This resurrection has been manifested by our Savior Christ Jesus, who abolished death and brought life and immortality to light." Kind of heavy-duty phrases? Basically, this says we have not sinned; therefore we do not need to BE saved as religions believe.

Why? Because as Jesus showed us, there is no death only continual life. Let's talk about Jesus for a moment. Contrary to the belief that he is God, needing to be worshipped as such, in truth we are all god, in our individual right, which he was attempting to teach us.

Jesus was an ordinary man. He came here, keeping his Oneness, his consciousness clearer, more connected to the Father. Then the renewal of the mind makes a complete transformation of the body so that every function works in divine order and every cell becomes incorruptible and immortal.

The resurrection is an organic change that takes place daily in all of us who are conforming their lives to the regenerating Truth of God. The resurrection takes place here and now in all of those who conform their lives to the spiritual law under And then we move into the larger love, beyond human love, the universal love where all who do the will of God are fathers, mothers, brothers, and sisters. So, Jesus didn't die on the cross to absolve us from our sins.

He was showing us that, there is no death, we already have life, light, immortality, and LOVE. The resurrection was to show us that we could all do that, because which it works.

we are also all divine and our work is to resurrect or ascend into the higher consciousness of God, in our physical body, mind and emotions.

And every Easter is a chance for us to accomplish that. So, to connect here, we have the solstice, which is time of balance, rapid change, and of moving into and out of form. New moon, time of new beginning, experiencing magic and miracles. Easter, time of ascension and resurrection.

The process which is raising all parts of us, spirit, soul and body into the Divine Christ consciousness, the Oneness that we are. Now one more piece, the astrological sign for this period. And that is Aries, starting the 21st of March, the beginning sign of the astrological calendar.

Let's look at another definition of Aries. The keyword description for Aries is "I AM." which is about developing a right relationship to self and understanding one's true identity. And because this is one of the 12 schools to work through, everyone experiences these aspects during this time, not just the Aries people.

Questions to look at are these: Is your identity in your personality, body, what you do, or the content of consciousness? Or is it the "I", the consciousness, the chooser, the soul, the spiritual being that you are? Are you developing a right self-image and self-concept?

Are you developing spiritual leadership? Remember the Son and the Holy Spirit description, are you bringing forth your ideas? As we ask who we are, we can start by understanding who we are not. We are not our thoughts, feelings, emotions, impulses, desires, energy, physical body, personality, what we do, and our roles and so on. What we are is a consciousness, as God is a consciousness. We are a center of pure awareness, with nothing in it except the content of our consciousness.? We are the chooser, the "I", the Soul, the I AM Presence, the Spirit/ Christ/ Buddha/God/ the eternal self.

That self is using all these energies in this evolutionary process to realize God/Oneness. Even though we have not realized it, we are the soul of God, and it is this process of initiation, resurrection, ascension, and higher light Body integration that we are all going thru. That helps us move into that form.

Another process to help us understand this is the 5 elements that are all part of Spirit—ether, air, fire, water, and earth. Let's start with Ether, the highest form of air, which is symbolic of our thoughts and connection to the heavens.

Then we experience fire, to burn off all negativity, to be with God. Then we go to water, which again relates to our emotions. connecting to the feelings of Spirit. And finally, we connect to the earth, which is our body, of which we gave total control of and connect to the body of God.

A master who has achieved this resurrection or enlightenment is recognized by their willingness to give everything to everything. How can you hold back when the whole universe is giving to you every moment? When it happens, your heart explodes.

After ascension when you look upon others now, then you see only the Beloved, for you know that only the Beloved exists, and your praise is unmatched. And you have learned the language of the heart, of Love itself. You are that LOVE now!

The instant this occurs, the first thing you say to your Self is: How could I have not seen this before? It is the most obvious thing in the Universe. It is definitely a special time to celebrate. Take time to feel and experience all the energy that is available to you currently.

Let all of what I have shared with you soak in. Know that you are special, divine BEINGS and allow yourself to be 'THAT I AM.' And awaken your Heart to yourself, to all, to LOVE, to ONENESS. Take the time to do that today after you read this lesson.

NAMASTE, I Love You and You are Loved

# Namaste Center Talk
# 11-02-16
# Lesson 16
# IDENTIFYING GRACE AS IT FLOWS THRU US

*Accept their reverence due to the Holiness walking with you.*

In this moment, I Give All Glory to God!! Here is today's Heartfelt Blessing. "You learn to speak by speaking, to study by studying, to run by running, to work by working; and just so you learn to love God and man by loving. Begin as a mere apprentice and the very power of love will lead you on to become a master of the art."— St Francis De Sales

Beginning today, commit yourself to mastering the art of unconditional love. The more you love, the better you live and in mastering this one art you become the master of that which is most important to you, your life. As I have told you before, I am a dual ordained Minister.

I am first an ordained Minister of Metaphysics, and recently completed my 2-year program from the Beloved Community and am now an ordained Minister of Spiritual Peacemaking. As your Minister I will be giving talks based on Metaphysics, Spiritual Peacemaking, New Thought, and other aspects of God's Love.

Today I am going to include Grace as a part of Peace. Grace is defined as: seemingly effortless beauty, ease, and charm of movement, proportion, or form. Peace is defined as: a state of physical or mental tranquility, calmness, serenity, the state of harmony between people.

Learning to be a Spiritual Peacemaker is all about BEING, not about DOING. It has nothing to do with what we say in the world or how we act. Those are natural DOING acts of who we perceive ourselves to be in every moment. Being connected to who we are BEING is more important.

How many of you have wished for Peace, either in the world or in your own lives? When we accept Peace as the single reality of our lives, we become natural Peacemakers on our own. It's not thru effort, it occurs naturally. Since everything is vibrational energy, a resonance field grows around us, and people fall into it naturally.

It's not about creating anything, but falling back into what has already been created, what cannot be changed. That natural aspect is inherently a part of us, and who has it been created by? God, of course. Peace is naturally within us as a part of God and that is what we fall back into, our essence, our truth.

And so is GRACE defined as the effortless beauty of our movements through our lives. The Course in Miracles says: "Nothing real can be threatened, Nothing unreal exists." Herein lies the Peace of God, not the Peace of humanity, but the Peace of God, that we are always searching for.

St. Francis said: "Our only job is to bring peace to everyone, and only when it is necessary, to use words. So, the words we say to each other are secondary. That's not where it begins. The words spring from a place within us, when needed. A place that is inspired by who we are. It is the way we live our lives, the way we are to one another. That is the real teaching and ultimately what is important. When we can identify what something is, then it is easier to build on it as opposed to something happening and we are not aware of it. Have any of you experienced situations like that?

We need to know what feels like magic, we have a reference point. If we can have a reference point of what it means to have the flow of Divine Grace thru us, to have it to touch, teach, and heal us, then we can really know how it feels. This is an essential place to come from.

Results are important because they reflect our mind. They reflect how we perceive ourselves to BE, what we perceive the world to be. For instance, when are we having thoughts in our minds that do not constitute PEACE? Or when are we having thoughts of judging others?

When are we having thoughts of fear? Lack? Look at all the thoughts that were negative and the corresponding results whirling about this past week. And how many of them really had to do with PEACE as compared to competition? Our results come from our belief systems, which come from our thoughts.

IF we want UNCONDITIONAL LOVE with the corresponding PEACE and GRACE, then we need to see a shift in consciousness and a shift towards Peace. What we need to know is that this is a shift that occurs naturally by choice. Choose to BE the peace.

A thought to have right now is that you can become a garden of Peace. It comes from having a deep YES to the path of God, a deep surrender to God. By saying, "Let me shine, let me be your vehicle here." you can then see everyone as the Christ, the Beloved. Know inside that "I am the Christ—so are you."

By being this, it allows the souls of others to feel the same. And they can really change without knowing why. Everyone's feelings of being lost from God can shift, just from your BEING. There is the one thought that affects us all, our so-called belief of separation from God. Why, does this shift happen?

Because we are all ONE and can feel what others are feeling. We are all affected by others' beliefs called mass consciousness. Therefore, it is time to see every moment of life as your ministry. Whether it is at the mall or at work. Every time someone comes to you, say YES.

"I am the Christ; you are the Christ" Be present with it. Feel the grace flowing thru you. We just need willingness to see the Beloved in each other and the situation. That is why you are here, to have your own ministry of PEACE. When you don't feel who you're wanting to BE, just go with the experience. Practice over and over. People can connect back to you, because of the energy change. They can feel it, be deeply moved, and not know why. They can say, I don't know what you have done, but my life has changed. DO this to the homeless, your enemy.

Hold the space that you are the garden of Love. The core of this is the willingness to see the Beloved in every situation. We don't need to have it all the time, but the willingness is all that is needed. Keep trying and remembering as often as you can. So, God can wrap the grace around you.

When you see the Beloved in others it affects you because you are doing what is true. As soon as you see it, a shift happens. If you say YES and go into the presence of Love, no matter what's happening, change occurs. Life looks and feels differently.

It's the first YES, committing into the energy and love of God into the true Christ presence, which allows you to see it in everybody.

It's the first YES, letting go, going into the LOVE. It is the power of living in the YES, staying in it.

When saying YES, everything changes; thoughts, words, and actions line up. Don't be afraid of it. If we don't stay in it, the flow of grace stops. The magic of miracles that is occurring around us all the time stops. Continually say YES, every morning, every moment.

When you say YES, let go of what it's supposed to look like. Our egos don't know what it looks like, though it believes that is does. Only God knows what it looks like. It is living in the WHATEVER, or SO WHAT of enlightenment (a phrase teenagers like to say that we can learn from).

I would like to know what it will look like, but I can't. Ask yourselves, have things ever turned out the way you planned? Actually, they have been better, so SAY YES, WHATEVER! And allow it to BE. Awareness is important of what you are doing in the moment. Don't judge yourself if you are in the NO of doubt.

Just feel it to see the difference and choose constantly the YES! When you set a higher intention while doing, a resonance field is set around that situation, bringing in more connection. If doing something for the Universe, the Universe rises to greet you there. Look for no resistance, look for the flow.

IF resistance is there, let it go, i.e., in your body, feeling illness, let it go, because the prescription of pain is due to programming, patterning. As a Spiritual Peacemaker you are holding the space for all the other humans on the planet; they can feel the connections.

We have so learned the process of Doingness. Now time to change to BEINGNESS. How about Believing and saying this statement: "I AM All that I AM," a glorious Light Being. A multidimensional melody of harmony and color expanding across the Universe and the outbreathing of my creative urge.

Would you believe that when you start saying it? No, but it is a start. We still believe that we must prove our worth by DOING. We need to change it to BEING. Know the DOINGNESS comes from BEING. In talking to others, saying what you want to say, asking for what you want.

Remember: it's all about the BEINGNESS - HOW WE HOLD OUR OWN HEARTS. How we love ourselves and one another. Lose the need to defend yourself. Stay in your truth no matter what anyone says around you. No matter what ever happens around you.

Keep in the peaceful place and GRACE flows thru you in abundance. When you come from the truthful, loving place, everything is o.k. You won't need words, knowing that you are in alignment, saying YES. A Course in Miracles says: "If I defend myself, I must be attacked."

We need to know that the attack is ultimately coming from ourselves. The truth within me does not need to be defended because it cannot be threatened. If you don't feel it, pretend and practice to look for the Beloved in others. The more I see it in others, the more I see it within myself and vice versa.

Never be afraid to extend your Love!! This is a Course in BEINGNESS (LIFE.) God is all there is, God is all there ever will be!! Prayer: "Heavenly Father, Mother God, I am made by Love, in Love, with Love, for Love to express the greatness of my unique Divinity.

I let my ego fall in love with my true essence. I choose to make a positive difference in my world. I let myself be captured by God's

Great vision of Oneness. Today I am in the flow of Divine Love, Peace, Tranquility, Unity, and Grace. I set myself free of judgment and unforgiveness.

I am at peace in my heart with all people. I walk in the Love of God, and through me, God's Love is made manifest. And so, it is. "Beloved Ones: It is time to BE the Peace, the Grace that you already are. Take this day to experience the effortless beauty, ease, and charm of movement OF GRACE.

Take this day to experience a state of physical or mental tranquility, calmness, serenity, and the state of harmony between people OF PEACE.

NAMASTE, I Love You and You are Loved

# Namaste Center Talk
# 7-25-09
# Lesson 17
# LOVE MAKES THE WORLD GO ROUND

*The Holiness transforms from its gentle light all things into its likeness and its purity.*

In this moment I Give All Glory to God. And to start, I believe God wants you to know that love means never having to say you're sorry. Erich Segal said that, and he was right. God loves you unconditionally, and that is why you never have to say you're "sorry" to God or anyone. Remember, God is in everyone.

If you love someone, relieve them of the need to apologize to you for anything that they are BEING or DOING. The need for an apology is the signal of a person who is mistaken about himself or herself. I AM on a mission to help people stop saying I'm sorry and it happens everywhere I go.

The biggest place for this is the grocery store. People come around the corner of an aisle and stop and say I'm sorry and I always ask, for what? Just say hello." A lot of times people say," you know I say that way too often." And I replied, "everybody does it, So, now you get to observe more when you say it and change it."

Just recently I bumped my cart into a woman, and she apologized to me. I asked her why and she said, "I'm used to it."

This is all about stating love for everything and how fear gets in the way. An example I share in my workshops: There is a young woman whose father left at birth. Now the energy and DNA of both parents are in the fetus, so she felt the empty space when born and the masculine energy wasn't there.

Later her mother remarried, and this male was there in physical form but not emotionally. So, she felt more loss of that male energy and at some point, because of the pain inside, created an emotional belief that men weren't there for her. And of course, carried that mistaken belief inside the rest of her life.

There was a young man who dearly loved his mother. She ended up being sick a lot and he wanted to take care of her from his love. As with all children who feel the pain in their parents and then create a thought around it, so did this young man.

He began to feel more and more responsible for his mother's illness and worked at trying to heal her through his love, but it never worked, so he took on a mistaken belief that his love hurt women. And of course, he grew up carrying that thought inside.

So, guess what? This young woman and this young man met each other as adults and fell in love and created a relationship. Things were going o.k. for a while as it was a relationship of the first stage of attraction, which was fun and felt good because of explored possibilities.

And then it became time to move into the second stage of power struggle when distrust from unresolved past manifests and it's time for inner work. Of course, it started with the young lady whose belief of men not being there for her expressed itself.

She would erroneously believe that this young man was not there for her and then withhold her love. The young man would feel that and then his old belief, that his love hurt women, would be activated.

And when she pulled away, he blamed himself and then he pulled away to not hurt her.

In this stage people start testing each other on who is going to get their way. And as that creates fear and conflict, she decided to leave the relationship as usual blaming men for not being there for her.

And then of course, his old thought came up believing that his love hurt women and of course, he didn't want to do that, and he left the relationship. And they both experienced the second stage that many relationships never move beyond. And they both got to feel right but unhappy about their beliefs.

The other choice, being wrong and happy. This gives you an idea of how and why many relationships fail when they operate out of old mistaken beliefs learned from their childhood. And I believe this is what relationships can be used for, to help heal those old beliefs and move deeper into partnership and love.

"It's love, it's love, it's love that makes our world go round, it's love that makes our world go round." Those are words from a beautiful song, but so very appropriate to help us live better lives. If we can only remember those words as we go through our lives each day, we will only have great days.

Let us make a promise now to start and end each day singing those words. We are taught that whatever we focus on or keep our attention is what we will draw unto our experiences. Let us pause now and ponder these words. What is love? Love is an idea in Divine Mind of Universal Oneness.

It functions in man as consideration, cooperation, unselfishness. When practiced properly we love despite and not because of. We will love everything unwanted right out of our lives. As we remember to practice love only, we will express more of our divine nature.

"Let brotherly love continue. Be not forgetful to entertain strangers: for thereby some have entertained angels unawares." (Hebrew 13: 1, 2)

Treatment/Prayer: Love is all there is, for God is all there is, and God is love. I AM love, for I AM God's expression. I live, move, and have my being in the loving consciousness of God. When I hear the still, small voice within beckoning me to follow, I know I AM being called forward into greatness, I embrace any fear.

I trust in love; I AM divinely guided. Obstacles appear and I may stumble; yet I stay on track I know love is all there is. At times the path may seem hard and steep. No sooner do I remember it is only an appearance that Love sweeps across the land. Hard and steep is transformed into ease and grace.

I AM returned to love. Every time I release and turn to God, I AM set free to be the love that is me. I AM the love of God expressing. My heart is filled with gratitude for this rich blessing. I give thanks, as I Know this is the truth. And so, it is.

NAMASTE, I Love You and You are Loved

# Fellowship of Spirit
## 4/21/13
## Lesson 18
## CHANNELING GOD

*As you step back the light in you steps forward and encompasses the world.*

In this moment, I give all Glory to God. Note these words of Christ in the New Testament which contain a great mystical truth: "I speak to them, not in the words of men, but in the words of Spirit." Spirit, as Christ referred to it, meant God. In effect he was saying that it was God speaking through him.

The Jesus part of his personality ego mind was set aside so that Presence or Spirit could speak directly through him. So, we can look at that statement as Jesus channeling God. And since this book is about the Love of God within, we may need some deeper understanding of channeling and what it means for us.

We have a lot of questions, and statements about channeling. Some people think it is a hoax while others totally believe in it and even claim that they channel certain beings. The practice of channeling became popular in the twentieth century. People would gather to hear words of wisdom.

They believed these words were spoken, supposedly, through higher beings, gods, goddesses, spirit guides and angels. They were looking for deeper answers to their questions of life, such as Who AM I and Why AM I Here and any help they could receive. Questions that are still being asked now—the need to understand that the information came from outside of them from some perceived being. The people doing the channeling had a shared belief, that what was being channeled was from a source other than God. This, of course is contrary to the beginning statement as the channelers claim to be mystics.

Mystics are people who deem their contact with God as the most important thing in their life. Because of this, they have no interest in spending time being a channel for other entities. A true mystic knows that thru their contact with Source, information revealed by channelers of other sources is much less in vibrational energy.

In addition, and most importantly, a mystic coms to realize that over a course of time, through inner contact with God, they become channels for God. That can be hard for people to understand, talking to God, really? This may be the reason for channelers to contact other beings, it's more acceptable.

When asked though, a mystic will always give God or Universal Mind credit as being the Source. Spiritual lecturers or teachers sometimes present material that is straight from Source, or God, but will not reference God. An audience will simply respond by believing that they are hearing a very wise person.

But the truth may be that the individual speaking may be hearing what is being said for the very first time, as they are spontaneously being used as a channel by God or the Universal Mind within. The same applies to the written word, such as this book, which I know is coming from Source.

God may reveal to the writer spiritual truths of which the writer was recording. These writings are read by another person, who may simply think that writer is spiritually brilliant. And that leads to people putting this person on a pedestal, as we humans do, not realizing it was channeled.

Remember Jesus' words from the New Testament, "Why call ye me good? IT is not I but the Father who doeth these good works?" I have to say that in my sermons and my work with clients. I was so surprised and blessed by God or Universal consciousness speaking through me.

We know that even Jesus, in his highly exalted spiritual consciousness, would not take credit for the wisdom that poured from his lips. He knew it was God the Spirit, Universal Mind he was channeling.

The main point to note here Beloveds, this is a book of tools and techniques to help you connect to God more, if that channeling is possible. If you doubt that you can do this, the truth is that any person committed to God through mystical mediation can channel God.

One of Jesus's truths that shows us what we can do is when Jesus said, "Even greater things than I, you shall do.'" So certainly then, channeling God is possible. In truth there is but one Spirit in this universe and manifesting as everyone.

Now for those who channel other entities, that information is specific to your own spiritual needs, but the Information channeled by others may not be precise regarding your own spiritual situation. This information may be colored by their own biases or judgments that have not been cleared out.

The question to ask is do you want less information for your situation, or do you want to channel and hear God yourself?? The question needs asking so that you can learn firsthand from within you what information or knowledge Source wants you to know that specifically pertains to your own life.

If you choose this mystical direction as your pathway, and you are genuine, sincere, and committed to the pursuit of Presence, some time without warning, you suddenly realize you are channeling the wisdom, love, and humor coming through you.

NAMASTE, I Love You and You are Loved

# Fellowship Talk
# 7/04/21
# Lesson 19
# "OUR JOURNEY OF FREEDOM TO LOVE"

*I walk with God in perfect holiness.*

In this moment, I Give all glory to GOD. Dear Beloveds, Happy 4th of July today. An important date for our country. We all know what this holiday stands for, so I don't need to give you a history report of its beginning. We talk about the 4th representing freedom and we need to understand it more.

Many people don't feel free for whatever reason. We could look at all the people in jail or even those not in physical jail, but still feeling imprisoned of some sort. Also, I have seen t-shirts with the statement "Freedom is not free." That is mistaken, as freedom comes from GOD, if we choose it.

That is the answer for all of us about anything, go to GOD/LOVE. I have mentioned before that one of the definitions of freedom is: Liberty from Undesirable states of BEING! That is powerful, meaning that it is always YOUR choice. "LIBERTY, doesn't that word just sound good?"

We are not in prison or locked up except by our own doing. That means that we can have freedom by changing our thoughts and emotions and BEING connected to the Christ consciousness within, the Love we are, not the undesirable state of fear.

We all have numerous life events that make us feel trapped and we desire to move out of them to freedom, however we would experience that, and then to LOVE. And since we are all ONE, what

I go thru, so do you in your own way. Which is why I titled this "Our Journey of Freedom to Love."

Let's start with me sharing the 8 steps of what Freedom first. And then talk about using these to help you create your life with Love.

1) Freedom is: Conscious Living: AWARENESS of BEING. "The substance or essence of an existing person." The Divine, Worthy, Loving Being of how we were created. And that is God who lives within us, and expresses thru us: I AM the Soul, I AM Divine, I AM the Mighty I AM Presence, I AM God's Will made manifest on Earth.

2) Freedom is the ability to see life as progressing, doesn't matter what the past is, nor the future. If we are too worried about the past, it blocks us from seeing life as progressing. Same when in the future; we can't enjoy the divine moment.

3) Freedom is Not Being Afraid to BE afraid. Learn to face your fears. To be impeccable: is to have a conscious understanding of your fears. It is important to know your fears, so you will know if they are yours or someone else's.

4) Freedom is Being Fully Engaged IN LOVE without Attachment. This of course means to engage in anything in life without being attached to the outcome. When we are attached, we put ourselves in a prison. We want to unconditionally Love self and others fully without expectation of it coming back in a certain way.

That is important. The answer is to BE engaged in Love, to BE and DO, because you want to. The other thing to look at is: what does fully engaged mean? To do something with all your attention and intention. To open your heart, to experience Love no matter how many times you have felt hurt. To BE in your car (vehicle) and be fully engaged on the highway of life.

5) Freedom is: Consciousness of Serenity in all of Life's Unfoldment. Life is either a daring adventure, or it is nothing. We are here to experience, to learn and to grow. And all-around LOVE self and others from Divine Love. If we knew how to do that and practiced it daily, we would be on our way to creating serenity in our lives. That's because if you were always failing, you might give up. But remember, it is by failures that lovers stay aware of how they're loved or loving. Life has pleasures and disappointments, and God is not found exclusively in either one.

6) Conscious exercise of One's volition, Opportunity to BE the Presence of God within. We are talking about BEING, which is our substance or essence of the Presence of God within. We are talking about a Conscious choice in exercising that choice.

7) Freedom is the Understanding and Conscious Use of Spiritual and Natural Laws of BEING. This states that there are laws that run the Universe and laws operating our state of BEING. The biggest being the Law of Attraction. It states that everything is energy; therefore, all our thoughts and emotions are energy. Each one vibrates at a different level, only attracted by matching vibration. There is only the ONE Mind, LOVE. There is no separation in the Universe. Only the One mind.

8) Freedom is the Ability to choose the Right Path for Oneself—To make Your Life a Blessing for Self and Others. Buddha taught about the 8-fold path of Life—Right seeing, Right Thought, Right Speech, Right Action, Right Living, Right Effort, Right Will, and Right Meditation, which tell us our freedom is

guaranteed through our relationship to God. It is freedom to deep unconditional LOVE thru BEING in our heart of Love.

NAMASTE, I Love You and You are Loved

## Namaste Center Talk
## 9-15-09
## Lesson 20
## OUR JOURNEY OF LOVE

*I light my mind, I light the world.*

In this moment, I Give All Glory to God. LOVE is the answer. Love is the right answer. Love is the only answer. Love is the state we desire to be in always. That is the LOVE of God we desire and deserve and to experience that which we need to move into freedom from those undesirable states of fear.

The reason BEING we can experience Divine LOVE and all its aspects. And we also need to learn to BE that which we need to BE to gain more healing and freedom to allow God to do his work. So, what I am sharing with you today is mostly about what I AM now going thru for my inner growth and since we are all ONE, this fits for you also.

There are a lot of changes happening on this planet. That is why I said OUR JOURNEY. And this lesson is about moving through freedom to LOVE. To accomplish that I need to heal all of myself to experience the freedom I need to get to Divine Love.

I have a connection with some of the Ascended Masters. One of them who has communicated with me more recently is Sananda, or Jesus. He has explained some things to me during this time about what this lesson is all about. Sananda and the I AM Presence (SOUL) assist in one's healing process to move thru freedom, healing body, mind, emotions, and spirit, therefore healing occurs in all 3 bodies.

On the spiritual level there are many multiple layers of the healing that is taking place and cannot be explained in just 1 word or with 1 phrase or understanding. It does not take place in a linear way. It is not just 1 dimensional or 2 dimensional, it is a multidimensional transformation. The healer within me and everyone is being awakened, further activated, and further empowered to the next step and the next level. We will be feeling more and more freedom which comes from connecting to the feminine energy, now being very much awakened as a part of that within us.

For every soul and spirit carries both the feminine energy and the masculine energy and both are always present and always needing to be in balance. And it is my feminine energy that is being tapped into right now, that is being allowed to flow, helping us to slow down, becoming more mindful of everything in and around us and not just everything that is said and put out thru our words into the world. Time to BE more mindful of all the energy that we put out and bring in, BEING more mindful of the receiving.

This is what we are to understand a great deal more about. Sananda is here to speak about that which our I AM is still gaining further understanding of and to speak about to us about that which we still do not have the full insight and clarity that we need. But that is coming to us and is meant to come thru our healing, freedom journey right now. And that is the sacred divine feminine power energy that is meant to flow in us freely and is meant to be in harmony and balance in every way in our life.

The feminine energy is the receptive energy, the receiving force, the receiving flow of energy. The masculine energy is the giving, the out flow, and the active force. And this is another thing we are being given the opportunity to fully embrace in every way and open, open, open our ability and potentiality, and power and gifts by receiving.

Allowing is also part of the feminine energy. When we allow ourselves to receive, we are working with 2 different parts of the feminine energy in a way that the feminine energy flows, manifests and helps us to allow healing, allowing ourselves to receive help, allowing ourselves to receive support.

There is still more to learn about this, Beloved. There is still more progress for us to make in this regard. And one of those steps in allowing yourself to receive, is being very clear in our communication and the use of our throat charka about what we need. And yes, very important in all of it, is feeling that you deserve it and that indeed you are worthy, which you are 100% by our birthright as a divine child. A child of the Light, a child of unconditional love, completely worthy and deserving in every way.

And don't let the ego ever convince us of anything other than that ever again. That is a great deception that the ego uses to try to stay in control. But it's time to see also our part of the ego is also being healed as you do the inner work required for moving on the journey through freedom to LOVE.

If there is one thing that a journey like this does, it humbles one. It immediately facilitates as this healing process and journey of releasing and turning away from those ego aspects that want to act in charge and BE in charge and it makes it so much easier because then we are required to surrender. Surrender has both a masculine and feminine function. There's the letting go aspect of surrendering when we literally must release, release, release, and then there is the allowing part of surrendering, the letting go part, the releasing part that requires the masculine flow of energy.

It is then then that the receiving part of surrendering is felt, which is allowing things to BE and then allowing us to trust, which is the feminine aspect of surrender. When both are in place a complete transformation of the ego happens, necessary for all that we feel that we are told to BE and are being called to do. If the ego is not the one leading the way or making the choices or decisions for all the healing and our ministries work, then yes, we are being called to BE and being further empowered to do.

Then, that cannot be the ego making the choices and decisions, and the acting and the leading must be the heart. So does not only illness lead the ego to surrender to the masculine and feminine aspects, but it allows the heart to open, requires the heart to open even more than it was before and to go there.

This is the greatest gift of all and in all that we have been experiencing, the opportunity is provided to go into our heart. Our mind has always and will always be strong, that is a great and powerful gift that we have. Like the tin man in The Wizard of OZ who had a gift that he had inside and didn't know it.

But this journey is so much more than a healing journey for the body, as I said. It is also the healing journey for the mind, emotions, and the spirit. All the 4 bodies of the Christ. And for the spirit, this journey is ultimately a journey into the expansion of the heart. Further opening and coming from the heart, speaking from the heart, living from the heart, choosing, and making our choices from the true will of the heart, knowing from the heart, trusting from the heart, discerning from the heart, feeling from the heart as this is far and beyond our ability to empathically connect.

This is something very important for everything we want to do, all the parts of our ministry work, for it to flow and to connect with God/Spirit. This is a service to allow us to BE the instrument thru which the Divine works, and the Divine will be done.

It comes from the heart, thru the heart and flows from there with great empathy, great love, and compassion. Not only is this increasing our empathy, but it is also increasing our compassion and our love. We always have had in our ministry work thus far the vision and knowledge that we needed, so much of what we needed was in place.

It is this heart connection which will move and flow from the heart and increase our compassion, empathy, and our ability to give and to receive compassion and love from the heart and back to the heart, that is now added to all that we know in our vision making the world a difference.

We always have had a big heart, a caring and loving heart. This is an expansion and the opening and a clearing away that which holds us back from speaking directly from the heart. It has always been easier for us to speak from our mind, knowledge, and intellect and we always will continue to do so. The capacity to do so will improve because of all of this. And there's the speaking from the heart and yes, allowing that which is being received in our heart to flow thru us and express out from us.

This is allowing that divine energy and all its forms of expression of masculine and feminine to be received by us to flow thru us and be expressed out from the heart, thru the heart. The throat chakra is the expression center but the energy from the heart chakra must flow out directly from the heart itself. It needs to expand, extending outward in the way the heart chakra touches others uniquely and not like none other of our chakras can.

Also, the energy from the heart flowing up and out thru the throat chakra, speaking from there, expressing from there, healing from there. It is not meant to be just expressed thru our words and our words only. It is also meant to flow down and out through our hands.

Even though the throat chakra is the chakra from which we speak, it is also our energy center of every form of expression in existence. Any form of expression of every human being that is capable energetically, is possible as the energy of the throat chakra, because of the role the heart chakra plays.

It is the center for all divine expression and is meant to express thru us, not just thru words and words alone, but also thru what is coming from our hands and thru our hands. As I said in the beginning of this message, awakening the healer within us is part of what is going on.

There is also an awakening of the direct energy of the Holyoly Spirit, the Divine Spirit, to flow from our heart thru our arms and thru our hands to all cells of our body. There is so much energy beginning to activate and flow now, so allow it. Right now, we can allow it to flow thru our arms and our hands back into our own body, connecting our hands together in the prayer position over our heart chakra, invoking the divine energy to flow thru us and to flow thru our hands.

With very specific prayers of intention, quiet the mind, connect to the heart and begin to feel the energy flowing thru our hands, and putting our hands where they are needed on our body. Not just throat chakra, but the heart and crown chakra which are opening significantly as a part of this.

If we allow, truly allow ourselves to receive all the help and support that is available for the full opening of what is taking place, then the full opening of your crown and heart chakra will receive what flows in directly from the Divine source and directly from all that I AM connected to.

That would be all of our I AM presence we are connected to—the incredible group of higher beings, all working with us. We will accomplish all we are to do and BE in our work. Do not forget to ask for that help and support. This is for all others to focus on that in their life.

NAMASTE, I Love You and You are Loved

## Fellowship Talk
## 02-14-14
## Lesson 21
## IS IT LOVE OR FANTASY?

*All the minds which God created are with me.*

In this moment, I give all Glory to GOD. As people come together to form a relationship, they most likely do not have any concerns as to whether the relationship is based on love or fantasy. And that is because they are more connected to the first of four stages of relationship called Attraction.

This is the stage where the couple has a desire to learn more and wanting to share oneself. It is a time when positive possibilities are felt and explored. In other words, the relationship is fun, and feels good. The couple is so caught up in this fun that they do not stop to ask, is this real or is it fantasy.

We have been told by different teachers, musicians, and others over the centuries that the greatest thing is Love. And when we feel it, we understand the Truth of it, as love is the most wonderful of all human experiences.

No matter the life experiences, deep within our soul, we know there is something stronger and eternal which is this aspect called Love. Since it is strong and eternal, then it is the LOVE we deeply desire. But most of the time we have no idea how to create it in our relationship.

The more we understand how Love is so important to us, we realize there is only One life in this Universe and that we are in union with what we call God. Love is the experience of unity; where we begin to know that God is Love and when we connect to that Love, we experience Oneness with God and our partner.

Once we comprehend the need to experience this Love as humans, we really want more. Then we begin to know that love is an expression of the Presence of God in all the universe. We open our hearts and begin to sense a natural desire to experience this Love in our life.

Then we embark on a frantic search to find love, no matter what. After getting a taste of what love feels like, we become driven for the need to have it in our lives. And that is where we can create problems as we often make the wrong choices in partnership.

Enormous numbers of broken hearts and broken marriages attest to this fact, with the growing percentage of divorces. Because of this happening, we need to slow down and really ask ourselves and pay attention to how we feel as to whether a current relationship is love or fantasy.

As I wrote in the last paragraph, with the percentage of failed marriages, over 50% and climbing for 2nd marriages, we should ask if most marriages are not based on love but rather, on fantasy. Now you ask, how can I tell whether the relationship I'm in is fantasy or the real Love.

To understand the difference, let's start looking at issues that most always appear in relationships causing them to be fantasy. First, we need to know that all relationships are for learning. Because of the union I mentioned earlier, we need to know that one partner is always a reflection of the other partner's mind.

That may be difficult to comprehend at first. This means that an opportunity for learning and self-mastery is available if we stay awake to it. Referring to the stage of attraction, it is a Spiritual law which states that you will attract people, places and situations that match your vibrational energy. Or in other words, people that correspond to your unconscious beliefs and expectations, unconscious meaning below the level of awareness. And where do these beliefs and expectations come from? They are formed in in our early childhood by being absorbed from our parents and the culture we grew up in.

These would include such things as religion, school, family, etc. We accept anything as real that was modeled. Early childhood represents our primary relationships education. Modeling is the primary form of learning. Unfortunately, most people had poor models for successful relationships.

As an example, if our parents continually struggled with money, then we just believe that is the way it is, and we subconsciously create the same struggle in our lives and primary relationships. We grow up modeling and creating relationships based on the one our parents had with each other and with us as children.

We have three bodies; physical (communication), mental (creation), and emotional (feelings and attraction). From age 0-7, we all live in our emotional body experiencing everything that goes on around us. Then our mental body makes an emotionally false decision about what we feel. And because the emotions are painful and the thoughts are negative, we store them in our body to feel safe, which is not the body's responsibility, and we forget about them until they come back up in relationships.

Since everything is vibrational energy including our thoughts, emotions, and actions, we walk around connecting to people, bringing others to us based on the Law of Attraction. While you are looking for a romantic relationship, you are recreating the personality type of your models.

In other words, because the mind thrives on the familiar, you may create a partner who is the same type as your mother, if you are a man. Or the same type as your father if you are a woman. And those are very important relationships that need to be paid attention to—mother and son, father and daughter.

Obviously, you may have some of each parent in your mate to work on. To the degree that you didn't succeed in your relationship with your parents, you're not likely to succeed in your relationship with your mate. And you cannot usually surrender into a deep level of intimacy with a partner.

You will teach your partner to treat you the way your models did as a child and vice-versa for them. Remember I wrote earlier that one partner is always a reflection of the other person's mind. That means relationships are for learning about oneself.

As we move forward in this relationship of difficulty for many varied reasons, we tend to blame or attack. These are the two worst aspects in a relationship. It's now time to do some inner work with you and your partner. When the emotional body senses upset, the physical body of communication sends out pain in all three bodies leading to illness if not dealt with.

ILL stands for I Lack Love, by the way. Once our physical body communicates the pain it's carrying, the relationship body (yes, your relationship is a body of communication) of both of you gets activated. And since this is all unconscious, we move into the 2nd stage of relationship, Power Struggle.

And you need to know that you have been living in fantasy and it continues if you don't do the work. In this stage, each partner starts testing the other, who is going to get their way and when. Around this time, your unresolved past rears its ugly head and you start feeling distrust of yourself and the other.

Remember, they are a mirror to you of these fears, as you are for them. And the struggle continues through many different Tendency's. One of Decision, where you make decisions from the altered ego out of harmony with your higher self. Look for an opportunity to correct your mistaken decision.

One of Projection, where you unconsciously place on others your own undesirable ideas and actions. Another one of Control, which is the degree that you feel the need to protect yourself, you tend to control others and circumstances out of fear.

Then the one of Suppressed Feelings, which practically everyone experiences as we are taught as children to stuff our emotions. When you do this, you create situations that activate suppressed pain to heal unresolved pain from the past, you stuffed in your body as a child. The body wants to heal itself.

Then we experience Retaliation, which is not confronting and expressing your anger or sadness in an appropriate way. You then express them at your partner, and many other tendencies. I've learned and taught my clients that an appropriate way is to really "feel" your emotions as you did when a child.

That is, scream in your pillow, have temper tantrums to release anger. And when feeling sadness, lie down let the emotion take you over and cry deeply. When you release in that way you can come back to the relationship and express yourself in a more positive way.

Many relationships never move beyond the second stage to the next one of cooperation of trust and working together. As I wrote earlier, over 50% end in divorce. Those relationships begin in fantasy as to what could be, but never get to real love because of not doing the necessary work.

Then it's time to discover whether you are creating the relationship based on Real Love or fantasy. Your Higher Self is motivated by Love, the altered ego is motivated by fear. People in upsets tend to look at the events and then blame and attack the other person. But the events are not the problem, decisions are. Because the mind does one of two things, either drawing in evidence to support the conclusion or changing the decision. When you do the internal work to change your own decisions about yourself and relationship, the external changes.

Then you move into the third stage of cooperation; sharing power, valuing each person's unique abilities, learning how to communicate thru any upsets that occur, thereby resolving them. Then you move to 4th stage of synergy and oneness, extraordinary satisfaction, intimacy (in-to-me-see) and deep trust.

When you wake up emotionally and are attuned to your higher self, the union with your choices, actions and results are the reflection of your higher self. Therefore, your thoughts will reflect what you really believe, the words you express will be consistent with your thoughts. And then your actions will be in alignment with the other aspects, and you will begin to live from your higher self, attracting to you a divine partner, someone on the same vibrational level.

As a Course in Miracles says, "Nothing real can be threatened." Therefore, anything that is real is lasting. It also states: "Nothing unreal exists." Anything that is not real cannot stand the test of time and will come to an end. Time to answer this question for yourself, is the relationship Real Love or fantasy?

If you come up with an answer that feels right to you, and you're willing to do the work, then the correct answer to this question will allow you to take the necessary steps to respond in a positive manner, especially if you are aware of God's inner guidance.

If you haven't already been meditating and connected to GOD within about this relationship, then the insight of whether it is love or fantasy will not come into your awareness. This practice will help you connect to your Higher Mind aspects such as loving, unified, peaceful, abundant, harmonious, and real.

Contrary to our common belief, we need to know that real love begins on a spiritual level. If it is real love, then know that God brought your soul and that of another together. For problems are challenges meant to stimulate further spiritual growth and the love you have for each other.

When you work on these issues with your partner you will begin to feel the power of real love beyond belief. To correctly discern whether you are experiencing real love, as opposed to fantasy, consider this, fantasy is based on need. Real love is not.

The needs of fantasy include, but are not limited to, sexual desire, financial security, emotional security, acceptance, position in life, power, or fame. In other words, fantasy is based upon what you can get from the other person. Real love, on the other hand, is based upon what you can give the other person.

This is because you love them so deeply, you feel it in the very depths of your soul. Fantasy is based on fleeting beliefs while real love is founded by God on lasting reality. The more you meditate, and connect with the Beloved, the more you turn your life over to GOD, the more sensitive and aware you will be spiritually.

The more spiritually sensitive and aware you are, the more you can sense what is in another person's soul. If you are in love with the inner beauty you have found in the other person, and they are in love with their inner beauty they have found in you, the likelihood is that it is real love and not fantasy.

As described earlier, the very essence of Love, real love, is being able to share that Divine Love by first opening your heart and then opening it to another person's heart, which is occupied by God. Therefore, we connect to the union, the Oneness and Trust that we inherently are.

That kind of trust is a spiritual trust. It is a sacred trust between two hearts, both containing God's Presence. And that kind of trust is a true sign of real love. Blessings to all on your relationships.

Namaste, I Love You and You are Loved

# Fellowship of Spirit
# 10/27/13
# Lesson 22
# I AM HERE FOR YOU!!

*This day I accept myself as what my Creator made me to BE.*

I give All Glory to GOD in this moment! I AM here in this physical body at this time because I chose to. I AM here at Fellowship of Spirit as the Minister because my Creator brought me here. I AM here in my life because my soul is here to grow my connection to Source to provide service to you and others.

I AM here to express ALL that Spirit gives me to express. And I AM here to help all of you and others create your Oneness with the Christ Consciousness and attain your dreams. And I AM here to help you all be healthy, wealthy, One with Source thru all the tools I have that Spirit has given me.

And I did not choose this spiritual connection and understanding consciously. It took more than that to bring this about. At times while it was developing, I could feel something powerful within, I would think, who, me? Not George Harris from the farming town of Sterling, Colorado.

Not the person who went through the abusive childhood and survived, or the person who was married and divorced more than once and other judgments I carried within about my life. But I kept going, listening to that inner voice of God and there were times I felt like stopping, wondering what it would be like if I went back to the way I had been. Thinking that it was simpler than the hard inner personal work I found myself doing. And thru all my work, I realized that you don't get to choose your spiritual calling, it chooses you.

And while you can quit your job you can't quit your inner calling. And then along with that, I learned that WE diminish God when we hold back our gifts, because God is within. We need to honor the Goodness and the Godness that we are.

There were three main tools as well as others that I learned to use for my growth, that you can use to allow your calling to manifest. So, this lesson is called: "I Am Here for You." The first step of opening to God and creating your desires is to step into your willingness to BE what you desire to BE. I have mentioned this before, and a way to do that is to say "YES." I learned to say YES to everything that came my way, everything that God led me into, and I continue to say Yes. That is an important foundation of how I came to being here at Fellowship.

First, to let you know, I never wanted to BE a pulpit minister. My first ordination was as a Minister of Metaphysics because I wanted it to support me in my consulting business working with couples and families. Then I completed a 2-year Seminary of Spiritual Peacemaking program and was ordained as a Minister of Spiritual Peacemaking.

When I came home after the retreat, I asked GOD, what was I to do with this ordination as I already was a Minister and I was told to just wait and BE, don't worry about doing, which is a message I was aware of and had practiced before: BE-DO-HAVE.

This was close to the end of June, and I just performed my work feeling what BEING a Minister of Spiritual Peacemaking was like. Then around the beginning of August I asked God when would I start

DOING something? I was told to wait, something big would happen. O.K.

Then the 3rd weekend of the month as I was at my New Thought church, I received this message from God: "It is now time for you to have your own church of 200 people. You will teach all that I have taught you. You will help people become Practitioners and Ministers."

Well, I had no church, didn't even want to be a pulpit minister, and didn't know how I would make this work, but just said O.K or YES. A week later, a woman who was the director of a small spiritual center whom I had met months earlier and agreed to come talk there in November called me. She told me the next week's speaker backed out and could I speak to them. I of course said YES, and I wanted to do a workshop. Then she said she wanted me to do a talk on prosperity and abundance as they were looking to put out a call for a Minister.

"Bingo!" I said, I just received a message a while back that I AM to BE a Minister of a church. She said that maybe it would be this one and she talked to the board, the congregation liked me and so I was hired. The interesting thing was this church was 4 hour's drive away from me and in a different state.

I would never have found that if not for God. That was the big thing I was told earlier would happen. I was the pulpit minister for three years before the Minister and founder of Fellowship of Spirit, this church, whom I had heard of before and he had heard of me, asked me to lunch. He told me he and his wife were moving to Argentina later in year and wanted me to speak there one Sunday a month. I changed things at my current church and spoke there. The congregation liked me and the messages I gave and kept coming once a month.

Then he told me they were moving to Belize and wanted me to take over Fellowship. I, of course, said YES and the board voted for me, and as you know, I became the pulpit Minister of Fellowship, my second church, the next month. Now here I AM the Minister and teacher, all because I said Yes.

This all happened after saying I never wanted to BE a pulpit minister. My mind could never have figured this journey by itself as God knows what needs to BE done. So, it is time for you to step more into saying YES to your life. To begin for you, it is necessary to turn your I don't know into a YES.

Turn your apathy into YES, Your I AM not sure into YES, your doubt into Yes. Begin to FEEL the energy of YES. YES, I CAN, YES, I WILL. Even add to it, I AM OPEN, I AM READY. Especially if you don't know where it's leading you and, trust me, most of the times you won't.

When you do this and say Yes, you are giving permission for the seeking to emerge thru you. Something to remember, "That which you are reaching toward is also reaching out toward you, as everything is all ONE." You are saying YES to your higher self, to give you the steps to move forward.

Nature uses a birth canal to bring about new life. So, if you're feeling squeezed right now in your life, it is because something is seeking to be born thru you. Growth is never easy but is always fruitful and worth the work. Saying YES leads you into wondrous places that you could not have figured out with your mind.

It is time to see what great gift is seeking to emerge in each of you today. Say yes and BE awake to your growth, your life. I have been through the pain and upset sometimes called the dark night of the soul and I learned how to move beyond that and create more in my life.

All of this was about receiving from my Source, and I have had to deal with ego doubt coming up. It stills does at times, as I continue to step deeper into my connection to God and therefore expressing myself out in the world more.

But the important thing to me with this ego upset is to keep turning it over to GOD, to have Faith and Trust and to keep saying YES, because I know how that helps me. The second aspect of my spiritual growth has been Intention as a strong guiding force.

The Intention process is from the "Intenders of the Highest Good," created by Tony Burroughs. The steps are: To intend to change, to intend to hear God more. To intend to receive what Spirit has for me and to choose or intend to BE what I came here to BE.

I have Intended to BE the best I could BE, a Master Integrated, Full Spectrum Teacher, Healer and Minister that integrates all Source has taught me. And to learn how to work on all 4 bodies necessary for total healing. I took these on much deeper in myself when I realized the path that God was leading me on.

The Intention Process is simple to understand and incorporate. All you must do is say, I intend and then follow it up with whatever you desire. It could be anything! You could intend to have a new car or world peace. Since there are no limits on what you think about, there are no limits on what you intend!

But I would say the biggest thing to intend is your Oneness with Source because everything comes from God. "Seek ye first the Kingdom of Heaven and All things will come to you," since we are all one. And that is what we are working on here at Fellowship and intending to create a wonderful, joyful life.

How about getting up every morning and intend that you are joyful and happy? How about intending fun and laughter? Intend that you are in perfect health, rejuvenated, aligned, balanced, and feeling physically great all the time. How about intending that you are always guided, guarded, and protected?

Start with some personal life intentions every day. Then look around at your life to see what you need. If the computer decided to go on the fritz, intend that it gets fixed. If you feel something going on in your body, intend that it is healed. If it looks like you are lacking some money, intend that you are prosperous.

Don't leave anything out because there's no reason to hold back! It helps you with your deeper connection to Source and receiving God's Love. You could also make a few intentions each day about your personal traits. For instance, intend that you are a more compassionate person. Intend that you are more kind or gentle. Sometimes, especially when there are a lot of dramas going on all around me like what has been happening with the pandemic, I intend that I see everyone in their highest light and every event from its highest point of view.

That way I'm able to observe all the sorrow and suffering in the world and remain uplifted. It is a way to not get caught up in life "out there" and to experience more peace "inside" your life. You can intend to remember that it doesn't do you any good to drop into someone's challenges and become troubled along with them.

It's much better to set an example by staying happy and cheerful. After intending for things like this for a while, you could take a closer look at the world at large and make a few intentions for it too. For example, intend that men, women, and children everywhere experience grace.

Intend that peace and harmony blossom across the land. And intend that this Earth is living in its highest light, and that, within our environment, the air we breathe is clean and crisp; the water everywhere is crystal clear and delicious; the soil is abundant with lush growth and beautiful fruit is dripping from the trees.

Intend that the animals are honored and respected; people all over the world are happy and smiling because they're being given everything that they need! And, finally, intend that all your thoughts, words, and deeds serve the highest and best good of the Universe, yourself, and everyone everywhere.

That is being the LIGHT Worker in the World. That is intending your life and then holding with intention how the world is and watch it change. As I have mentioned before, it is time for all to remember why you came here and an explanation of the 3rd aspect.

Let me remind you that many of us are realizing that we made an agreement before we came into these bodies that we would come together at a certain time to bring light and love onto this planet and to usher in a golden age. Some have forgotten and some just have a feeling, like an inkling of a long-lost dream, that there really is a reason for us to be here now.

In either case, on one level or another, we are all experiencing a movement toward looking at life from a perspective of having made agreements and arrangements to come here and meet with other souls and soul groups. Then we can join so that we can assist in raising the vibration of this planet.

This is what is being remembered at this time; and it is this movement which will, in fact, bring the golden age into manifestation. And we are ALL a part of it and WE here are growing into it. And the more you open to the purpose of why you are here, will help you and everyone. All of you as members of this Fellowship are here for that reason and I was brought here to help you remember and join in creating the life we are all meant to have. I AM here for you. Here is an intention for you to say: I intend that I am discovering and Being and doing what I came here to do."

Join me in the non-conformist oath: Repeat after me: "I intend to be different; I intend to BE Unique; I intend to BE the Light in the world. I intend not to repeat what other people say." I hear a lot of you here state how you feel Love and Spirit in this building, and I love that because I know we all are allowing the Light to shine thru us even stronger. Also, I hear comments about fear of growing this center and losing the connection and the closeness we have. I want to share with you why I wouldn't allow that to happen.

This center is important to me, as you are important to me, to my personal/spiritual growth as well as your personal/spiritual growth which is why I titled the talk I AM HERE FOR YOU. As a friend reminded me this past week, I am here to tend the flock.

And that is because of the three vows I took when I was ordained as a Minister of Spiritual Peacemaking. The First Vow: To love all beings unconditionally. This is the summation of the teaching and mission of Jesus to demonstrate unconditional love. The Second Vow: To hold the Divine Feminine in my heart until it is time to give her back to the world. The Third Vow: To feed the sheep of God. These are my intentions as Minister of Fellowship of Spirit, and I ask you to join me and watch what we create through God's Love.

By vowing to feed the sheep, I recognize that my own salvation is intimately linked to each person I serve. When one is freed, we are all freed. Where is the logic in that statement? If you think with your mind, you will not find it, but if you gaze softly with the heart, it will appear before you as if through the mist.

That is why I have been led through all that GOD directed me by saying YES. I have gained the skills necessary to help each of you in the ways you need and to be here of support if you get lost, no matter how big we grow. (I AM also here for those of you reading this book).

I know that our growth will be just right, because of all these three aspects, 1) Saying Yes, 2) Holding the Intention, 3) Knowing why we are here. All three are about GIVING LOVE and feeling LOVE. Therefore, we are opening to the title of this Book, which is "God's Love is All There is." And we need to connect to this truth when we are feeling the absence or separation of the LOVE of GOD deep within. And vowing to Love unconditionally. Think about this? Is God limited or unlimited? Is God healthy or ill? How about you? Time to wake up to these truths from God and watch what happens.

NAMASTE, I Love you and You are Loved

# Fellowship Talk
# 10/27/13
# Lesson 23
# "SEEING THRU THE EYES OF GOD

*My mind holds only what I think with God.*

I Give Glory to God in this moment! Let me share a reading from "Practicing Spirituality with Jesus" Course. BE THE EYES, FEET, AND HANDS OF CHRIST. Christ has no body now on Earth but yours, no hands but yours, no feet but yours.

Yours are the eyes through which you look out on Christ's compassion to the world; yours are the feet with which he is to go about doing good. Yours are the hands with which he is to bless men now—Saint Teresa of Avila quoted in "God Makes the Rivers to Flow" Sri Eknath Easwaran.

To Practice This Thought: Be the hands, the feet, and especially the compassionate eyes of Christ in your world today and every day. See the Christ in everyone. Our deepest fear is not that we are inadequate. Our deepest fear is that we are powerful beyond measure. It is our light, not our darkness that most frightens us.

So, we ask ourselves, who AM I to be brilliant, gorgeous, talented, and fabulous? Those words are the beginning of a speech given by Nelson Mandela quoting Marianne Williamson. I love those words because they are so true of us. This talk is about "Seeing thru the Eyes of God."

I have mentioned numerous times before that we are here to See through the eyes of God, which was a lesson in the Seminary of

Spiritual Peacemaking where I received my ordination. We probably question what "Seeing thru the Eyes of God" means.

First, it means that we are more than we believe ourselves to be. We knew this truth as children, because we knew that we were not separate from God or anyone. But then we took on fear from those around us and buried them inside and began our process of separation from God, and those fears became ours.

Not at first. We resisted because we knew inside our truth. But as the fears bombarded us over and over, and as we stuffed our emotions, and took on thoughts that we were less than, we started creating our ego. We slowly began to forget our truth.

And to this day, there are many of us, who are working thru old emotions of sadness and anger, around separating ourselves from ourselves and then from GOD, from our Source. During this time of forgetting we began to think we were our bodies, but we're not.

Yet, these bodies are the instruments that God expresses thru, as us, in us, and our bodies need our unconditional Love for every aspect of it. We began to think that we were our problems, because we believed in "separation "something outside of ourselves."

So, we have ended up identifying ourselves by being addicted to our problems. We began to think that we were our ancestors, because we took on the fears, the beliefs of our parents, who got it from their parents, who got it from their parents, and on and on.

We were also identified right at birth and during childhood. "It's a boy, it's a girl" and what those mean. Then other judgments such as: shy, quiet, boisterous, and talkative. Daddy's girl, tomboy, "so smart." That includes our thoughts around illness and prosperity.

As a healer, metaphysician, and Spiritual teacher, who knows our divine connection thru our body, I understand how strong the fear is regarding any of these life aspects. How it looks at times, as if there is only one choice. It is said that there is not an original idea, but just an idea looked at differently.

It is the same with our fears and negative beliefs. They are not new; they have been around since the time of creation. And we have been carrying them in our bodies as ours from our ancestors. We think that we are our identities. We use the small "I" in so many ways.

One time, I like chocolate, another time I hate chocolate. One time, I like getting up in the morning, another time, I hate getting up in the morning. All the time, thinking that it is still the same "I". One time, we say "I Love You" another time, "I Hate you."

And every time we say "I" we think that we are speaking about just us, but it is our different, small "I" s from our ego. In truth, there is only ONE BIG "I" -- I AM. I AM the CREATOR OF ALL THAT IS. With that "I," there is no separation, there is no out there, outside of ourselves. I AM THAT WHICH I AM, AND GOD IS THE TRUE BEING OF THAT WHICH I AM. No truer statements were said. We think that we are our bodies, our illnesses, or our desires, which are constantly changing. We think that we are our loves, our pains, our addictions.

But I tell you, Dear Ones, we are none of those. We have shortchanged ourselves too long, believing in our smallness. And it is now time to discover our true nature; it is time to express our Infinite Being. We are truly here to express the glory of God that lives in each of us.

We are here to balance our Spirit with our Will. And to begin this, it would help to understand that God's will is the same as our Will when we connect to our Divine nature. Not when we are listening to our ego, our small I, with so many parts. You want to understand how God sees you?

How to "SEE" thru the Eyes of God as the title of this lesson says. Let's go over some points.

1) God sees: We are a piece of all that is, sired by the LIGHT, (GOD) in order that "GOD" might experience itself, greater than it was before. That means that we are here to allow God to express itself thru us in its bigness and grow in its expression. Do you get that?

God wants to become greater than it was before, and it does that thru us. And he wants the same for us. That thought goes against my Catholic background that says God is already all-knowing. How powerful to now know that God is growing as we are growing, as the universe is growing. These fit in with the Law of Growth that I spoke about a month or so ago that everything grows.

2) God sees: We are the embodiment of a love so vast, so incomprehensible, that we run from its power. Yet that power is what we are. Do you get that?

A love so vast, that we can't even comprehend it all. And yet it is inside of us, it is us. That power of Love. And if we were to break down the letters of the word LOVE, it could stand for Luminous Organism Vibrating Eternally." That is, YOU.

3) God sees: We are the higher power that is greater than ourselves.

Wow, did you get that one? We think that there is a higher power out there called God that is greater than us. But we are that higher power. Heir to all that is. Try telling yourself that, the next time you have some worry or fear going on in your life, some little event that has you caught up in it. We are the higher power that is greater than our ego selves.

4) God sees: We are a portion of the infinite, a piece of God, destined to wake up one day and remember just that. And you know when that day is? NOW. This is the year, this is the time, RIGHT NOW. Not later, when my spouse gets their act together, or my children listen to me, when my friends treat me better. Or when I make more money, or any of several reasons we give for staying where we are. It is now time, this moment, to choose to wake up. And it is a choice, always.

Neale Donald Walsh, in his book, "Tomorrow's God", says: "We concern ourselves with the fear of whether we are loved, whether we will wake up to our power. In fact, ALL of you will awaken. Life is the process of awakening. That is why we are here in this school. It is the process of Becoming.

It is the process of knowing that one has become what one always was. It is the process of rejoining the inseparable, which simply knows that separation never occurred. We are ONE.

5) God sees: We are incomprehensible forces of energy, living for now inside physical instruments, because that is what we CHOSE to do.

Yes, Beloveds, we chose to come here and experience life on this planet, in these bodies, with our parents and all our experiences. That means that it is time to look at your life and experiences with gratefulness. Try saying those words more often, I AM GRATEFUL, I am grateful for Life, now and forever.

And you might say, how can I do that? There is so much pain. Well, that is what unconditional Love is all about. Loving every aspect of yourself, every aspect of your body, all your emotions. All of you. Not just some. Not just the ones that others approve of or the ones you like and keep hidden the others. But ALL of you, can you do that?

6) God sees: WE are a portion of the whole, therefore what God is, love is. How do you see God? In whatever way you do is how you see yourself.

IF you can accept that the world we experience is as we experience ourselves, it is only logical to then accept that we experience God as we are.

Deepak Chopra, in his book "How to Know God", defines 7 stages of God. And as God is in us, these are how we not only see God but ourselves. As you read these, see what stage you would place yourself.

Stage 1 - God the Protector, fitting the world of bare survival, full of physical threats and danger. (We still have people living that reality.)

Stage 2 - God the Almighty, fits a world of power struggles and ambition, where competition rules. (Still a reality.)

Stage 3 - God of Peace, fitting a world of inner solitude, where reflection and contemplation are possible.

Stage 4 - God the Redeemer, fits a world where personal growth is encouraged, and insights are powerful.

Stage 5 - God the Creator, fits a world that is constantly renewing itself, where innovation and discovery are valued.

Stage 6 - God of Miracles, fits a world that contains prophets and seers where spiritual vision is nurtured.

Stage 7 - God of Pure Being, fits a world that transcends all boundaries, a world of infinite possibilities. I AM.

I suggest you read this book for further understanding of the 7 stages.

7) God sees: We are power centers of unlimited magnificence, supreme intelligence, who have never been separated from our source, for we are that source. That explains a whole lot. Visualize being power centers, standing in full glory with God's energy, like electricity flowing thru you, and you BEING ONE with Source.

We could connect to the words that Jesus spoke: "The Father and I are ONE." Not the Father or the Son of the Father, but I AM ONE WITH THE FATHER. There is no Separation. That is You, that is Me. Remember the top 2 Commandments. 1) Love the Lord thy God, with all thy Heart and Soul.

As we understand more that we are One with God we see that to mean: If we Love God inside of us, therefore we Love us, with all our Heart and Soul. Or at Least we should. 2) Love thy neighbor as thyself. Well, once you love God within you, love yourself with ALL your Heart and Soul, then you love others the same.

We are all ONE, Beloveds, there is no separation. Earlier I mentioned about Infinite Being, which God is, therefore, so AM I. A little more about Infinite Being: Infinite Being is the all-encompassing consciousness from which the universe was created.

Everything in the universe is made of consciousness. Just as each snowflake is unique, so is each person. Each of you is part of the ONE with same qualities but we express them uniquely. Your primary purpose in life is to experience life, from one individual, unique point of view. Yours and God's. The reason individual souls exist separately is that each one is expected to develop its own character fully, and to shine its own unique light. But we are still not separate from Source. You are an expression of Infinite Being as it experiences itself from all possible viewpoints.

With Infinite Being, you can make the deepest possible spiritual connection, discover your infinite possibilities, become an expression of your true, inner self. Consciously transform your reality to BE-DO-HAVE all that you want and desire and deserve. You can SEE thru the Eyes of God.

Let's end by completing Nelson Mandela's speech: "Actually, who are you not to BE fabulous, gorgeous, talented, and brilliant? You are a child of God. You're playing small doesn't serve the world. There is nothing enlightened about shrinking, so that other people won't feel insecure around you.

We were born to make manifest the glory of God that is within us. It's not just in some of us; it's in everyone and as we let our own light shine, we unconsciously give other people permission to do the same. As we are liberated from our own fear, our presence automatically liberates others."

PRAYER: Everything is done for the Glory of God. Wherever I may BE, it is God who is truly present. Whatever I may BE DOING, it is God who is DOING. Whatever power I may possess, it is GOD who is the power. Whatever I may give, it is GOD who is truly giving.

Whatever I may learn, it is God's eternal silence filling me. Whatever LOVE I may have, it is GOD who truly loves. Whatever success I may have, it is GOD who has truly succeeded. And whatever

I am seeing, I am seeing thru the eyes of GOD. And so it is. Go out today and BE the light that you are, SEE thru the eyes of GOD and watch what happens.

NAMASTE, I Love You and You are Loved

## Fellowship of Spirit Talk
## 12/30/02
## Lesson 24
## NEW YEAR THOUGHTS

*I AM not a body, I AM free, for I AM as God created me*

In this moment, I Give All Glory to God. You have been growing into the Love you have sought. By flourishing and flowering, you have come home to yourself. You are LOVE personified. Everything is composed of energy vibrating at various frequencies, and that includes our thoughts and emotions.

Let's look at this a little deeper. God has said through Jesus, "What I do you shall do also and greater things than these shall you do." That means to me that we can have whatever we want in our lives. We are God manifested and have the same power to manifest in our lives.

In fact, we have done that in our lives already. And if we are unhappy with our results, then it is time to change our beliefs. Since our mind always goes to what's familiar, then we will naturally go back to the beliefs of being unlovable, not good enough or whatever thoughts we have carried for so long.

Especially if we have had failures in the past, it is difficult to see and accept that we can now have success. You have grown into the Love you sought. By flourishing you'll come home to yourself. You are love personified. Everything is comprised of energy vibrating at various frequencies.

Questions to Ponder. What and where is God for you? How does God's energy manifest in your life? What does God's energy physically feel like to you? Is your journey more externally focused or internally guided? Am I a kaleidoscope of fragmented pieces or a multilevel spiritual being?

What beliefs am I not ready to face or examine? Which costs more, to reexamine your thinking to change your life or live with pain and feel dissatisfaction? What matters more to you and what gives your life meaning? Are you settling for too little or asking for too little? What's next in your life?

The more you accept the incredible power to choose to change your thoughts, the more you can change your life into anything you want it to BE. Are you getting better than you used to BE? Let go of Ego and let God do God's work. Stay focused on what you want rather than what you don't want.

Are you a hardworking, trudging climber or have you felt Spirit's guiding energy boosting you into a synchronistic fashion? Spiraling into the Light is God's love attracting us into the One Source where all this is comes to know Itself as unified, whole, perfect, and complete.

Then we are pulled through the veil to awaken as emissaries radiating the light, to know God as us. What matters most to you and what gives your life meaning? Are you settling for too little or asking for too little? Before you do anything ask, "Will doing this bring more gratitude, peace, love, or joy?"

What parable will you share when you are "living proof" that your spiritual processes have made a major difference in your life? Jesus said: "What I do, you shall do also and greater things than these shall you do." Which pathways and what challenging ideas will you choose to explore next?

Are we enlightened beings, or do we experience enlightened activities? When we emerge our inner and outer ways to BE into one seamless whole, then we will know what to do to have what we want, and possibly receive more than we expect. We can stop functioning in reverse, struggling to survive.

The more you accept this incredible power to choose to change your thoughts (since they are all vibrational energy attracting to your situations matching their vibration), the more you can change your life into anything you want it to BE.

It may be time to let go of ego. Who wants to live in fear and a life of less than? Let God within you do God's work. What do you want, more love in a relationship, more creative expression of yourself, a job or career that fulfills you? It is time to stay focused on what you want rather than what you don't want.

And don't separate your wants, focusing on one and letting the others go. Put them all together in a new expression of your total life. Any step you take towards something ask yourself, "will doing this bring me more gratitude, peace joy and love?" If so, go towards it. You will then discover the powerful manifester that you are by having your life be all the joy, love, and passion that you have desired all these years.

Namaste, I Love You and You are Loved

# Fellowship of Spirit Talk
## 2/22/15
## Lesson 25
## A MOMENT OF CHRISTHOOD

*How does energy manifest in your life?*
*I feel the love and light of God within me now.*

In this Moment I express God in all its Glory!!! I have shared information about "Practicing the Presence" in numerous talks and a workshop I created. All the lessons, of course, were very important. But the last ones were great, as they helped tie the information together. I wanted to share that information with all of you for a deeper understanding of what we are doing with Practicing the Presence. I have talked about the great moments in life we have and that we need to release the past and stay connected to the moments now, the moments of Christhood.

The correct letter of truth necessary for spiritual unfoldment is embodied in the 7 principles as set forth in Practicing the Presence. They are:

1) "Love God with all your heart, soul and mind acknowledging that God is the only power and that there is no power in any effect.

2) Love your neighbor as yourself by refraining from all judgment as to good or evil, by forgiving seventy times seven, and by praying for your enemies

3) Recognize the infinite nature of individual being, the understanding of which is, that there is only one Self.

4) Begin to understand the realization that to him that hath shall be given; that means to pour out all the love you have to receive more.

5) Demonstrate God and not things; in other words, connect to the creator, not the creations.

6) Meditate on God and on the things of God.

7) And live only in this moment, which is the only moment there is.

"The Moments of Christhood. A full realization of any of these principles, living and working with them, day after day and week after week would be sufficient to transform any experience and usher us into the Kingdom of Heaven.

We are learning, of course, the kingdom is inside. And I will give a talk in the future expanding upon those 7 principles. Instead of attempting to grasp the full meaning of truth in the short span of a day or week, we should begin working with one principle.

Take that principle into meditation daily for at least a month, dwelling on it until its inner meaning is revealed, and it becomes a deep part of ourselves and then observe to what extent our words and acts are in harmony with it. Thus, the principle becomes settled as a deep part inside of us.

So, for the talk today, let's focus on the last principle: "Living Only in this moment, which is the only moment there is."

"The Moments of Christhood." If we are sincere in our desire to experience God, we shall make it a matter of decision to let nothing interfere with our firm resolve and steadfast purpose. There is a simple practice to help with this, and that is by developing a consciousness of nowness, a state of todayness. This state of newness is achieved by consciously training ourselves to live only in this minute, by recognizing first that we do not live on yesterday's manna.

Our responsibility is only for this day and for this moment. Whatever demand is placed upon us, let us fulfill it this moment. This practice of nowness develops a personal consciousness because there is nothing to do except what is at hand this moment which is being in a moment of Christhood.

And then, we are never worried about supply, not about any obligation due tomorrow. There is only today and only this moment. When "Christ livith in me," as the Bible says: when Christ lives my life for me, no demands are ever made upon me; every demand is a demand upon the Christ.

There is only the moment—a moment of Christhood. Yesterday does not exist. As a matter of fact, even an hour ago, even the last second does not exist. Our demonstration is to maintain our integrity to the highest degree to which we are capable at any given moment.

If each of us could begin every day afresh with the realization, "I and the Father are one," it would make no difference what our mistakes were yesterday if they are not repeated today. Which relates to the statement, "Go and sin no more." In archery meaning "off the mark."

Then, in this moment we are Christ-consciousness. And our lives are leading to our spiritual fulfillment. Let us hold steadfastly to this Christhood. We not only stand in our own Christhood, but we stand in the Christhood of every person. This life is not ours. This life is God's. We belong to God, and God is responsible for our life and for our fulfillment. When responsibility comes, let us be sure that we do not permit this human sense of I to come forth and say, "How can I accomplish this? How am I going to perform that?"

My strength is not sufficient; my bank account is not adequate." Jesus did not permit the word "I" to intrude when he was called upon to feed the five thousand. He acknowledged that of himself, he could do nothing. The moment we have a God-experience, we no longer live our own life; God lives Its life as us.

The moment we live this life of the Spirit, which is a sufficiency through Christ, none of the things that afflict the world will afflict us. In that moment we bring ourselves into oneness with spiritual law. That is the secret of spiritual living and the mystical life. "I and the Father are one and all the Father has is mine."

This constitutes righteousness; conscious union with God; the realization of God as support and supply; the realization that only God can love. To let God's love flow through us to man and then claim no reward for it because it is of God and not of us.

Now all those words are quite powerful and the whole principle sounds so empowering and yet I know as humans we have a hard time living in the Moment of Christhood. As the class states, it is something that we must Practice over and over. And to assist us, we need to surrender, trust, and be in gratitude.

So, let's talk about surrendering. In other words, Releasing Personal Ego Will to God's Will. The greatest act of pure folly in human life is to live by the will of one's personal ego. The personal ego, after all, is no more than a composite of limited knowledge and understanding.

The personal ego has no more from which to form its conclusions than the limitations of outer sense impression, learned knowledge from outside sources, and formal education—similarly based upon outside knowledge.

The problem with Outer knowledge is that even the most sophisticated science is subject to change, which means a truism of today may be tomorrow's fiction. Upon such flimsy criteria for being, the personal ego is founded. Therefore, when one's personal ego begins to expound on its will for one's life, it stands on mental and emotional quicksand. Whatever is hoped, wished, and prayed for, by one's personal ego, will and can, time and time again, turn out to be but a mirage. This leaves one in a mental and emotional desert, thirsting for a better life, but parched to the core.

Despite such disillusionment, the average person today clings desperately to this illusion that one's personal ego and its will must be the definitive decision maker in their life. Many people feel that if they give up the will of their personal ego, they will be left barren of all joy, and end up living an austere life.

They liken it to that of monks in a monastery. The truth, however, is quite the opposite. More of life's blessings become available as a greater number of opportunities become apparent. GOD'S PRESENCE takes over your life when you truly release your personal ego's will to the WILL of God.

Unlike the limitation of your personal ego's knowledge, GOD'S knowledge is unlimited in its Universal understanding and about you specifically. The will of your personal ego is based on half-truth—a limited view of what your life was meant to BE. On the other hand, God's view of your life is unlimited.

When you give up your personal ego's will, you begin to see your life through the eyes of God. You begin to realize that what is best for you has its foundation in your very soul. You live those moments of Christhood. You realize that only God know what direction your life should take. And how the greatest progress for your soul can be made in this lifetime. The Bible says: "He who loseth himself (personal ego and will) for my sake (Christ God-self) shall find himself (the true self and soul) one with Spirit of God."

People seem to think that if they give up the will of the personal ego, they relinquish their right to the so-called joys or indulgences of the flesh and human life. In reality, the only thing that is changed is that you see life's experiences with greater wisdom and are better equipped to penetrate with a discerning eye what has real value or significance in your life.

This does not mean that love, material needs, or other important factors of life are cast aside. It does mean that what is of significance in your life has an opportunity to grow and expand. It also leads to a greater possibility for enlightenment. Remember as I said a couple of weeks ago, GOD IS MY GOOD, MY GOOD IS MY GOD. Love is the answer, the love of God, the love of truth, and the love of our neighbor. It should be the function and the mission of those of us who Practice the Presence to reveal that God is only experienced in proportion as God is expressed.

Now carry this message in your mind and heart where you will always remember the principles; and in your heart, dwell upon the gift which has been given you, delivered to you from the Father —the gift of the realized Presence within you. Bless It always that It may increase.

Namaste, I Love You and You are Loved

# Fellowship Talk
# Aug 22-2021
# Lesson 26
# "Battle of the Wills"

*I choose the joy of God instead of pain.*

In this moment, I give All GLORY TO God. Beloveds, I have talked to you numerous times before about New Thought's belief that God is everywhere. There is no place where GOD is not. In fact, a friend has been asked if they believe in a God. Their reply is no, I believe in only GOD. Meaning God is all there is. I have in the past and I do it again point out that each of us is the Christ which is the energy of God. If you have a problem with those two words, that is your ego issue, use a word that fits for you, such as Love, Universe, or others.

So, believing that truth, I have identified each of you as the Christ. When we talk about God being everywhere, do we mean it? Or even understand it? We may see it in each of us and the other. What about the space in between us? How about in the seats, the walls, everywhere? Can you comprehend that?

We are connected to the ONENESS of Life. ONENESS with everything, we are not alone. This means that I AM, you are, everyone is connected to GOD's will, God's heart, God's Love.

Oh, I have mentioned that word GOD's Will. What does that mean since I'm talking about the battle of the wills?

Last year when the pandemic hit us, we all had more time for self, and I spent mine meditating and reflecting. One day walking down my path/driveway looking at nature, which there is a lot of in my area.

I was really enjoying all of it and talking to God and I heard God say, "I AM also in the pebbles on the ground, in the bushes and the trees.

Everywhere you look there "I AM" which means God/Spirit/Source is in all the spaces, between the spaces between the forms. Let's look at it deeper. When we talk in New Thought about Oneness, do we really understand it?

If God is everywhere and God is everything, then God is in everything around us as well as all the space in between; like health, prosperity, abundance, relationship and so much more. Health is not just in the hospitals, or doctor's offices or even just in our body. If God is everywhere then all these aspects of God are all around and can be connected thru oneness with God. Same with Prosperity/Abundance. It is not just in our pay checks or money received from work. It is all around us.

This means we can connect with health as well as prosperity/abundance by connecting with Source. Instead of just looking at the check book or bank balance, we can open up to all the abundance around us, seen and unseen, expected and not expected.

If there is no place where GOD/LOVE is not, then we can connect to healthy cells in our body thru healthy thoughts and emotions of God. With relationship, we can release negative thoughts and fearful emotions. We can connect to Love thru connecting to God's Self Love.

We can understand that LOVE is in everything all around us, on the planet and other planets, in our galaxy and galaxies beyond. Feel that, comprehend that, ALL is LOVE, ALl is GOD! Think of when a child is born, having been in the womb for 9 months or so receiving and having all its needs met just by BEING. It was a fetus, a soul, then being yanked out of the womb into this empty space, or so it seems. Then it gets spanked on bottom to start the breath, all of which might signify struggle coming out of the womb, abuse, and separation from its home that it has been connected to.

But there are people around to help, to welcome this being as a divine being coming into physical form. It's not alone. We could consider the same process as being breathed out of the heart, mouth of GOD, in the beginning with God.

The difference being that when that happens, we feel and know that we are still connected to GOD and all the LOVE and life and everything, and we knew it as God's Will of Love and Oneness. But then we create a battle of wills. As we are born in childhood, we become connected to separation, forgetfulness, pain, suffering and the rest, which is ego's will.

When did that first start? In the story of the Garden of Eden (which stands for all those in physical form at that time, meaning us and our fellow brothers and sisters), God showed them everything around them and said, all of this is yours, I ask that you receive and co-create with me.

Meaning that we had the power to create thru our thoughts and God wanted us to create through his Will. To create with GOD thru LOVE all that we wanted. But the humans at that time thought they could do better and separated themselves from Source.

And that was the beginning of the ego will, and it has run us ever since thru all its fear aspects. The Will of God is the path of "surrender." You see, without the Will of God, you will not go very far on your evolutionary pathway. This is the very first step, the first imitation that must be mastered before you can progress through all the other steps.

If you're not willing to surrender to the "greater will of your being," the Will of your own Divine Source, how will you ever find your way home to the realm of light. If you're not willing to surrender to that which is seeking to bring you all the way home to your divine perfection, joy, bliss and limitlessness, your lost paradise, how do you expect to ever get there? The Will of God is not a God outside you. It is simply that God that you are and that you always have been. Although when in physical incarnation you tend to forget temporarily that your divine Presence is omniscient, omnipresent, and omnipresent and can fulfill all your desires.

Aren't we told those are the aspects of God? You have temporarily forgotten that you are nothing less than an expression of this great I AM incarnated in human form. You are here seeking an advanced enlightenment and total spiritual freedom.

You are here to become an unlimited God in all planes of existence. This is an agenda of Love for the Self, and that Self is no one but you. Lifetime after lifetime you did not meet your goals for that incarnation. That is why you are still here facing many challenges instead enjoying the bliss of the light realms. Your God Self is calling you to "surrender" to the path that is laid before you, day by day with love and trust. That is what I had to do on my recent cancer journey. Remember the three aspects: Surrender, Trust, and Gratitude.

Through that loving surrender, step by step, you will be shown the way back to the "sun of your being" your divine perfection. Christ inferred that no man could enter the Kingdom of Heaven except by doing the Will of the Heavenly Father.

Spiritually doing God's Will is releasing yourself to God and the more you release yourself to God's Presence, the more that God rules your life, the greater the opportunities for you both personally and materially. When God's Will is guiding your life, you realize how very fortunate you are to be able to have released the will of your personal ego in favor of GOD'S Will for your life. Doing God's Will is not viewed as a sacrifice, but rather as an attainment of will that knows how to direct one's Life. Limitation and illusion (Ego's will) are replaced with UNLIMITED POTENTIAL and REALITY.

Your Consciousness is filled with DIVINE CERTAINTY. You have given your life to God, and he has replaced your uncertainties with Divine Certainty, so that your life is now being lived in the inner knowing of God's Presence within you. You are now living the Moments of Christhood and by connecting to the Christhood Moments you have a vision to Behold. Something else to consider.

In the beginning of the Edenic days, man was complete whole and harmonious, One with God. By the grace of God everything flourished and there was peace. What man is now striving to attain in his search for God Is the re-establishment of that state of complete peace and harmony. A state in which we are not at war with one another, but in love with one another.

A state in which we do not deprive others but share and give to others. But we have been looking in the wrong way and in the wrong places. All our desires will never be established by searching for some supernatural power, i.e., the 2nd Coming of the Christ.

Man needs to re-establish himself in this original state which is our oneness with God. Hundreds of years of frustration and failure should have proven to the world that it is not the work of a god to do this for us. It is our work to do this for ourselves by establishing the original relationship of Oneness.

The Master said: "Ye shall know the truth and the truth shall set you free." Nowhere does it indicate that it is God's responsibility. Jesus, through all his teachings never placed the responsibility of our sense of separation from God, upon GOD, but upon us.

To us is addressed the entire teachings of Jesus the Christ, to us is addressed the entire WILL Of GOD, not to God, to us. Lest we should flounder, however, the Master has given us the way, the where, when and the how of this demonstration of unity.

The way is Prayer; the where is the Kingdom of God within us; The when is now—the moment of Christhood, the how is BEING. With this understanding we come into a recognition not only that there is a God, but that God is the Inner Self of our own Being.

It is a God who is not separate and apart from us, to be worshipped afar off, but closer than our breathing, nearer than our hands and feet. The simple truth of the MASTER causes us to withdraw our gaze from upward and outward and turn it in the only direction in which we can find peace and harmony, God's Will within ourselves.

Then our attention has shifted from the outer to the inner. We can take the next steps taken by every great master: Ask and it shall be given to you; Seek me within; seek, knock, if necessary, plead, but always from within.

With that, I and the Father are One is no longer an intellectual perception, but, and this becomes a demonstrable relationship, visible in its fruits by living in God's Will. The Spirit within is unfolding, revealing, and disclosing Itself acting in and through us. God is Love.

No God can operate in our experience except through Love or God's Will. And we must become the instrument through which that Love is permitted to escape. Henceforth, the commandment "Thou shall love the Lord thy God with all thy heart and then thy neighbor as thyself," will have no significance as we are loving. There is no miracle God except the miracle that becomes evident in the living of our Oneness with God's Will. We have done our bit at creating a self beyond, but we have failed.

NAMASTE, I Love You and You are Loved

# Fellowship Talk
# 4/29/12
# Lesson 27
# "I AM A MAGNIFICENT, UNIQUE AND RADIANT ASPECT OF THE DIVINE"

*I AM the holy son and daughter of God itself.*

In this moment, I Give All Glory to God. I stated in the forward that I would be writing about Love and God as the 7th precept of Deepak Chopra's book titled: "How to Know God, The Soul's Journey into the Mystery of Mysteries," which is the God of Pure Being - "I AM."

Let's start with this powerful statement. I AM the divine image of God manifesting perfection in my life!! On Sundays, we take time thru our meditations, readings and the talks or lessons to go through all the knowledge taught from various disciplines down through the ages.

We need to remain awake to all the words from God out there to enhance our spiritual growth. That is from religion to philosophy, psychology, spiritual peacemaking, metaphysics, mysticism, and including help and insight around your communication and relationship skills that I provide.

That's because all these aspects, if they are put together and understood properly, can be a guide to us. I AM excited about this lesson that Spirit/God has given me for today because it is quite simple and simple is important to help understand the topic of Love.

And, because I really want ALL of you reading this book, to read more and take in for yourself what wonderful, beautiful, beings of

LIGHT and LOVE that you are. I have a friend who is a great artist. She mostly does soul drawings of people as well as spiritual artwork.

She did one for me awhile back and I have it up in my meditation room. I wish I could show it to you, but it says: "I AM A Magnificent, Unique and Radiant Aspect of The Divine." What does that mean? Let's first look at what it doesn't mean or say.

It doesn't say: I AM weak, I AM poor, I AM too tall, I AM too short, I AM not good enough, I AM bad, I AM overweight, I AM sick, I AM poor, I have a mean streak, I AM outspoken, I AM not loveable. I AM a sinner, I AM stupid, I AM alone, (Any more you can think of?)

NO, it says: "I AM A Magnificent, Unique and Radiant Aspect of the Divine" Again, what does that mean? Let's start with I AM, the words of God. Those words are found in so many places throughout the bible and ancient spiritual teachings. I will share 3 with you today.

1) We have been told that Moses was leading his people, the Israelites, out of bondage to the Promised Land. When he left his people to go up the mountain and talk with God, he was given the 10 commandments. God also talked to him regarding taking these people away from the Pharaoh. And also how Moses was to tell them that God would help his people. Well, Moses being slightly unbelieving about the whole thing, as we all would be, asked this question as quoted in Exodus in the Bible. (In those times people of great faith still had doubt.) "When I come unto the Pharaoh and the children of Israel and say to them The God of your Father has sent me to you" and they ask me "What is his name? What shall I say to them?" And God said to Moses, again quoted in Exodus, "I AM THAT I AM." This is what you will say to the Pharaoh and children of Israel:

"I AM has sent me to you." Now there is more to that phrase; there is a code in the name that I will talk to you about later. Part of it is I AM THAT WHICH I AM, and GOD IS THE TRUE BEING of that which I AM. (The Moses Code by James Twyman)

2) Also, "In the Beginning…. I AM." "So, God created man in his own image, in the image of God created he him, male and female created he them." Genesis. Therefore, we all have an "I AM" presence, our Masculine and Feminine Presence which is our soul connection to God.

"I" is ALPHA, the beginning, signifying the ONE, the Source, the Father. "I AM OMEGA," (the ending) signifying the Mother (represented by Mother Mary.) The Masculine and Feminine Polarity of God "I AM" is the beginning and the ending, the ALPHA and OMEGA of all that is. That is a very powerful explanation of our higher inner self.

3) When Jesus said: "'I AM the Resurrection and the Life," He gave forth one of the mightiest utterances that can well be expressed. When He said: "I AM," He did not refer to the outer expression (the body), but to the Mighty Master Presence—God within.

He repeatedly said: "I of myself can do nothing. It is the Father within— the 'I AM' — that doeth the works." That is why as a Minister, I always say some statement at the beginning of my talks such as, I GIVE ALL GLORY TO GOD!!! Again, Jesus said: "'I AM' the Way, the Life, and the Truth." By saying that he gave recognition to the One and Only Power — God in Action within him. Again, He said: "'I AM'" the 'Light' that lighteth every man that cometh into the world," prefacing every statement of vital importance with the Words

"I AM." Did you hear that? Prefacing every statement with those words.

That is why you must be careful what you say after those words, as they have power. Contemplating "I AM" as anything and everything, you wish to be is one of the mightiest means of releasing the Inner God Power, Love, Wisdom, and Truth, and setting it into action in the outer experience.

Again, let us refer to His mighty utterance, perhaps one of the greatest ever spoken into the outer expression: "'I AM' the Open Door, which no man can shut." Do you not see how very vital this is when you come to review understanding these Mighty Statements?

When you recognize and accept fully "I AM" as the Mighty Presence of God in you—in action—you will have taken one of the greatest steps to liberation. REMEMBER, when Jesus spoke of himself, he was also speaking of everyone. That means all the words spoken thru me are meant for all the readers also.

Not enough emphasis can be laid upon the importance of contemplating as often as possible the "I AM" as the Mighty, Active Presence of God in you, in your home in your world, and in your affairs. Every breath you breathe is God in Action, in you.

Your ability to express or send forth thought and feeling is God acting in you. Because of your free will, it is entirely up to you to qualify the energy sent forth in your thought and feeling and determine how it shall act for you. SO, we begin this statement as the title with 2 very powerful words, "I AM."

Now, the next thing to consider is what words do we use behind them? The negative ones above which come from ego, or the more powerful, positive ones that Jesus uttered. Our ego is that part of us that perceives itself to be separate from God and everything else. It believes it doesn't deserve anything, especially the fulfillment of your dreams. A well-known acronym for ego is "edging god out." How can we edge out the Creative Force of the entire Universe and still have what our soul most longs for? That ego forces us to fall backward and play it safe and never comprehend the infinite potential that lies within.

Even Moses' ego got in the way because he said to God in Exodus: "Who AM I that should go unto Pharaoh, and that I should bring the children of Israel out of Egypt?" And God may have replied: "Who are you not, to bring them out?" "WHO are YOU not to be big, to be all that you desire to BE.

Remember, I AM that Which I AM. That is quite a lot about the beginning I AM, I hope you really understand the important of those words. Let's go on with the other parts of this message:

1) It says: I AM a Magnificent...What does that word mean? It is defined as Splendid, Lavish, and Beautiful. Also, to arouse admiration and wonder. Splendid means: gorgeous, sumptuous. Are those words that you would use to describe yourself?

Think about the thoughts you have around LACK or SEPARATION. As I say those 2 words, what emotion are you experiencing inside of your body? Now change it to Lavish, Splendid. What feeling comes up in your body now? One that is more of abundance?

And, to understand that YOU, as the wonderful YOU, can arouse admiration and wonder to know that other people see that in you. This statement says the truth for you, so maybe time to carry that word around inside of you, MAGNIFICENT, SPLENDID, LAVISH, words expressing God's Love in you.

2) Unique....... what does that word mean? Being the only one of its kind, not like anything else of its kind, incomparable, rare, and unusual. The only One of its kind. Therefore, this world is unique because of you. It would not be the same without you. Even though we are ONE with GOD and each other, we are unique in our expression of Source within us. We all are expressing different qualities of GOD. There is no one else like you, rare and unusual.

3) I AM radiant!! What does that word mean? Radiant: emitting energy in the form of electromagnetic waves. Therefore, Light, a band of electromagnetic radiation which is related to its source. Meaning that YOU as the LIGHT is related and connected to Source, God, and Spirit.

And this radiation is considered as being a person's own rightful source of illumination. You're right to shine the LIGHT that you are. Therefore, you are a radiant, shining bright light, expressing great joy or hope. A point which is a source of radiant energy. Take that in Beloved's. YOU are a RADIANT LIGHT connected with Source. And therefore, naturally BEING that illumination that you inherently are.

4) Aspect. This means that what is said is part of you and you are a part of the whole of God or the whole of everything. Like the drops of water in the ocean, the grains of sand on the beach, the leaves of a tree. You are an aspect, a part of the whole, containing it in you.

It also means: Outward appearance, the direction in which a thing faces, Therefore, you could think about which way you are facing. Towards or away from your Source? What aspect are you of GOD?

5) Let's go to the next word, DIVINE. This means of GOD, addressed to GOD, having the nature of God, superlatively good or beautiful. WOW, those are some powerful words. So, what aspect of GOD are you? A DIVINE One. Again, think of yourself now as I say these words.

You are of GOD, having the nature of GOD, you are DIVINE. You are ONE with GOD, not separate as you have believed. All the problems you have created in your lives have come from your human miscreation's. They have come from forgetting our truth, being separate, living from our ego of fear.

Carrying around old, ugly, low vibration thoughts that we have expressed after the words I AM, as I stated in the beginning of this lesson. We are divine, and it is now time to live that truth. As we move into Ascension, which just simply means we are growing into or ascending into a higher level of consciousness.

We WILL BE MOVING within the 5th dimension, leaving the 3rd dimension, which will be connecting with the Christ Consciousness. That will be Oneness, expressing our soul and purpose for being—Our I AM Presence.

That is why these words are pictured with a butterfly. It is time for all of us to grow out of being the caterpillar and morph into our beautiful unique butterfly with wings to fly that is you, all of you, and that is LOVE. "I AM" VERY SPEICAL "I AM" special...in the entire world, there is nobody exactly like me.

Since the beginning of time, there never has been another person exactly like you. Nor will there ever be in the future. No one has my smile, my eyes, my nose, my hair, my hands, or my voice. "I AM "Special. In all of time there has never been anyone who laughs exactly like I do, or cries, or who thinks exactly like I do.

"I AM" special. "I AM" the only one, in the whole of creation, who has my set of abilities. Now, there is someone, who is better than "I AM" at one thing or another because every human being is superior to every other person, in at least one regard.... but "I AM" special.

And "I AM" superior to each other in at least one regard. No one in the Universe can reach the quality of the combination of my talents, abilities, feelings, heart, head, or hands. Like a room full of musical instruments, "I AM' a unique symphony Through all of Eternity.

No one will ever look, walk, talk, think, or act exactly, like I will. "I AM" special, "I AM" rare. In all rarity, there is enormous value. Because of my great value, I need not imitate any other person. I will accept, verily, celebrate my differences, because "I AM" special. And it is no accident that "I AM' special.

I must realize that God made me special for a specific purpose...He has chosen a job for me to do that no one else can do as well as I can. I have a divine plan as Jesus did. Out of the billions of applicants, only one is qualified. Only One has that unique, right combination of what It takes, and "I AM" that one, "I AM" special. "I AM" very special, AND SO IS EVERY OTHER HUMAN BEING."

"I AM a Magnificent, Unique, Radiant, Aspect of the Divine!!!!

Namaste, I Love You and You are Loved

# Community of the Beloved Family
# 1/2022
# Lesson 28
# MISCELLANEOUS

*I walk with God in perfect holiness.*

This section contains some more insight about Love that I couldn't include in any of the lessons, so I am including them here. The statements in Italics under the titles all come from Course in Miracles.

God has a way of allowing us to be in the right place at the right time. I was walking down a dimly lit street late one evening when I heard muffled screams coming from behind a clump of bushes. Alarmed, I slowed down to listen and panicked when I realized that what I was hearing was the unmistakable sounds of a struggle. There was heavy grunting, frantic scuffling and tearing of fabric.

Only yards from where I stood, a woman was being attacked. Should I get involved? I was frightened for my own safety and cursed myself for having suddenly decided to take a new route home that night.

What if I became another statistic? Shouldn't I just run to the nearest phone and call the police? Although it seemed an eternity, the deliberations in my head had taken only seconds, but already the cries were growing weaker. I knew I had to act fast. How could I walk away from this?

No, I finally resolved, I could not turn my back on the fate of this unknown woman, even if it meant risking my own life. I am not a brave man, nor am I athletic. I don't know where I found the moral courage and physical strength—but once I had finally resolved to help the girl, I became strangely transformed.

I ran behind the bushes and pulled the assailant off the woman. Grappling, we fell to the ground, where we wrestled for a few minutes until the attacker jumped up and escaped. Panting hard, I scrambled upright and approached the girl, who was crouched behind a tree, sobbing.

In the darkness, I could barely see her outline, but I could certainly sense her trembling shock. Not wanting to frighten her further, I at first spoke to her from a distance. "It's OK," I said soothingly, "The man ran away. You're safe now."

There was a long pause and then I heard the words, uttered in wonder, in amazement. "Dad, is that you?" And then, from behind the tree, stepped my youngest daughter, Judy.

# Prayer Treatments

## LOVE
### (Emmet Fox)

There is no difficulty that enough Love will not conquer

No disease that enough love will not heal

NO door that enough love will not open

No gulf that enough love will not bridge

No wall that enough love will not throw open

No sin that enough love will not redeem

It makes no difference how deeply seated may be the problem

How hopeless the outlook

How muddled the tangle

How great the mistake

The answer is always LOVE

# NEW "OUR FATHER"

Our Mother/Father God who are within,
Hallowed be our name.
Our Kingdom come; our will be done
Within as it is without.
Let us express this day.
Our daily birth right
Forgive us our judgments,
As we forgive those who judge against us
Lead us into the Light
As we deliver ourselves from fear
AMEN

(Written by Rev. George Harris)

I wrote this while taking some Science of Mind classes. It was the first time I learned that God was not out there somewhere but inside of me and others. Time to change this long beloved prayer to something that fits more with my new beliefs.

## **DEFINING LOVE**
### (Christina Tilla)

Love is a funny thing!
WE love as we Love -
The Love that complies us, moves us and cherishes us
Is the Love from which we came, and we give.
There are songs written of Love -
There are books, poems, movies, and tales of Love
Each defined by Itself.
Love yourself - for God's sake - Love yourself
Let it guide you, sustain you and nurture you.
For we know the absence of Love is nothingness -
For there is never such a thing. Love is
You can never separate Love from yourself
Any more than Love can be separate from you.
For me to bid a farewell to Love would be a lie -
Love cannot—It only can.
Love is the healer from which we all believed once
That the absence of Love has done harm or injury
When in the entirety of time, only Love existed all along.

# THE RHYTHM OF GOD
## Daily Meditation

Father, this is Your day, the day which you have made. You made the sun to rise; You have given light and warmth to the earth. You have given us the rains and the snows; the seasons of the year are Yours, seedtime and harvest, cold and heat, summer and winter, day and night. This is Your day.

You created me, I AM Yours. You created me in the womb from the beginning. Use me this day, for as the heavens declare the glory of God and the earth showeth forth your handiwork, so must I show forth the glory of God. This day let me glorify God. This day, let God's grace flow from me and through me to all those whom I meet.

Father, it is thy intelligence that I need today—not my limited wisdom, but my infinite wisdom. This day I need all the Love with which Thou can fill me. Give me thy wisdom and thy Love in full measure.

Father, I have great tasks today that are beyond my understanding and beyond my strength, and so I must rely on You to perform that which is given to me to do. You have said that You are ever with me and all that You have is mine.

Grant me the assurance today that Your Love is with me, that your wisdom guides me and that Your presence upholds me.

Your grace is my sufficiency in all things. Your grace! I AM satisfied to know that Your grace is with me. That is all I ask because that grace will be made tangible as manna falling from the sky, as a crude of oil that never runs dry, or as loaves and fishes that keep multiplying. Whatever my need, Your grace provides for it this day.

## PRACTICING THE PRESENCE
## (Joel Goldsmith)

Read this as a song as if God is speaking it to you.

Song: *How Great is My Love for You*

I have so much to tell you,

But I cannot say with words

How great is my love for you

And there is nothing to compare

In order to explain

How great is my love for you,

Not even the sky or the stars

Not even the sea and the infinite

Is greater than my love

Not more beautiful I despair to seek

Anyway to tell you how great my love for you is

Never forget not a second

I have the greatest love the world has,

How great is my love for you

Not even the sky or the stars are more.

Never forget not a second. I have the greatest love in the world

How great is my love for you

It is the greatest, strongest, truest love.

# CONTRACT

I LOVE FATHER/MOTHER GOD WITH ALL MY SOUL AND ALL MY HEART!!! FEAR is the only thing that keeps me from BEING totally committed to the path I have chosen for my life. I know that all FEAR is nothing more than a manifestation of the feelings of loneliness, separation, or rejection, specifically my feelings of being apart from God. I know that these feelings go away when I reestablish my awareness of my Oneness with God.

To ensure that awareness, I _____ enter into this Covenant with God. I agree to love the Lord my God, with all my soul and mind every minute of my life. I will always keep this vow in the forefront of my consciousness. I will keep this in this lifetime and it's my intention (personal vision) _____. (What do I intend to do on this earth plane while I am here, stated clearly and specifically. (That's my part of the covenant.) I agree to place God within me first and I agree to manifest my vision.

(What is God going to do?) God will walk beside me all the way, keeping me aware of who I am and taking away all of the thoughts and feelings of loneliness, rejection, and separateness BEFORE they even enter my consciousness.

In addition, God will provide all that I need to manifest my vision and provide abundantly.

A SIGN: I agree that this sign _____ will be a reminder of my covenant with God.

This is a binding contract between God and me that works. God will remind me of it every time I get shaky and begin to do outrageous things, because I know now that God and I are ONE.

DATE _____

SIGNED _____

PRAYER: Everything is done for the Glory of God. Wherever I may BE, it is God who is truly present. Whatever I may BE DOING, it is God who is DOING. Whatever power I may possess, it is GOD who is the power. Whatever I may give, it is GOD who is truly giving.

Whatever I may learn, it is God's eternal silence filling me. Whatever LOVE I may have, it is GOD who truly loves. Whatever success I may have, it is GOD who has truly succeeded. And whatever I am seeing, I am seeing thru the eyes of GOD.

And so it is. Go out today and BE the light that you are, see thru the eyes of GOD and watch what happens.

Love is All There is

# Rev. Dr. George Harris

# Books Published by Wise Woman Press

## By Emma Curtis Hopkins
- *Resume*
- *The Gospel Series*
- *Class Lessons of 1888*
- *Self Treatments including The Radiant I Am*
- *High Mysticism*
- *Genesis Series 1894*
- *Esoteric Philosophy Deeper Teachings in Spiritual Science*
- *Drops of Gold Journal*
- *Judgment Series in Spiritual Science*
- *Bible Interpretations: Series I, thru XXIII*
- *First Lessons from the Journals of Emma Curtis Hopkins*

## By Ruth L. Miller
- *Unveiling Your Hidden Power: Emma Curtis Hopkins' Metaphysics for the 21st Century*
- *Coming into Freedom: Emily Cady's Lessons in Truth for the 21st Century*
- *Power Beyond Magic: Ernest Holmes Biography*
- *Power to Heal: Emma Curtis Hopkins Biography*
- *The Power of Unity: Charles Fillmore Biography*
- *Power of Thought: Phineas P. Quimby Biography*
- *The Power of Insight: Thomas Troward Biography*
- *The Power of the Self: Ralph Waldo Emerson Biography.*
- *The Power of Practice: Emily Cady Biography)*

## By Ute Maria Cedilla
- *Mysticism of Emma Curtis Hopkins, Volume 1, Finding the Christ Within*
- *Volume 2, Realizing The Christ Within*

## *By Christine Green*
- *A Caregivers Journal*
- *Anatomy of Caring*

## By Cath DePalma
- *I Can Do This Thing Called Life So Can You*
- *Energize Your Creative Super Powers – 7 Ways to Spiritual Success*

www.ingramcontent.com/pod-product-compliance
Lightning Source LLC
Chambersburg PA
CBHW060656100426
**42734CB00047B/1958**